THE LORD OF THE RINGS

THE RETURN OF THE KING ™

PRIMA'S OFFICIAL STRATEGY GUIDE

Mario De Govia

PRIMA GAMES
A DIVISION OF RANDOM HOUSE, INC.

3000 Lava Ridge Court
Roseville, CA 95661
1-800-733-3000
www.primagames.com

ASSOCIATE PRODUCT MANAGER: CHRISTY L. CURTIS
SENIOR PROJECT EDITOR: BROOKE N. HALL
SENIOR DESIGNER: MARC W. RIEGEL
EDITORIAL ASSISTANT: KATE PASTOOR

ISBN: 0-7615-4394-5
Library of Congress Catalog Card Number: 2003111140
Printed in the United States of America

03 04 05 06 GG 10 9 8 7 6 5 4 3 2 1

Acknowledgments

Prima thanks Jonathan Harris and Nina Dobner of EA, and Chris Smith of HarperCollins for their help in the creation of this guide.

Contents

Introduction

The Fellowship of the Ring™ formed to save Middle-earth™ from the treacherous power of the One Ring. From the Council of Elrond in Rivendell, they set forth on their journey toward Mordor to destroy the One Ring in the fires of Mount Doom. Many challenges assailed the  Fellowship, from Ringwraiths to legions of Orcs to the fearsome Balrog that took the great wizard Gandalf the Grey from them. However, hope ultimately prevailed and the Fellowship kept true to its path.

That is, until the Fellowship split apart as they neared the dangers of Mordor. In the forests of Fangorn, Aragorn, Legolas, and Gimli met up once again with a reborn Gandalf the White and traveled to the lands of Rohan. There a great battle occurred at Helm's Deep between men and the wizard Saruman's forces of evil. To the east, the hobbits Frodo and Sam searched for a way into Mordor with the destruction of the One Ring in the forefront of their minds.

As the hobbits draw closer to Mount Doom, Aragorn, Gimli, Legolas, and Gandalf travel by various roads to Gondor to aid the men of Middle-earth in preparing a desperate last stand against the unspeakable forces of evil. Against the gates of Minas Tirith, they expect Sauron to unleash thousands of troops to quickly snuff out the hopes of all free people. To withstand the unrelenting forces of Sauron, the members of the Fellowship know the destruction of the One Ring is the only thing that can save them. Will Gondor prevail? Will Frodo and Sam make it to the fires of Mount Doom? In this final chapter of *The Lord of the Rings*™, the fate of Middle-earth is in your hands.

HOW TO USE THE WALKTHROUGH

The Lord of the Rings: The Return of the King—Prima's Official Strategy Guide is organized to give you fast and easy access to information you need. The walkthrough gives you the inside scoop on the path you'll follow, the places you need to go, and tips on what you need to do to progress in the game.

Walkthrough

In the walkthrough section of this guide, the numbers on the maps correspond to the numbers on the screens that come after each map. They point out such things as important items, landmarks to keep you oriented, and places where explanation may be required.

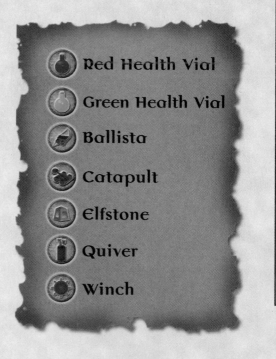

- ![] Red Health Vial
- ![] Green Health Vial
- ![] Ballista
- ![] Catapult
- ![] Elfstone
- ![] Quiver
- ![] Winch

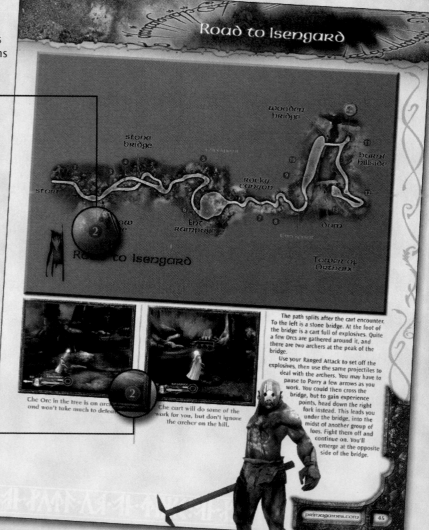

This guide doesn't outline each and every encounter you'll have, it does cover every path through the game. In other words, the guide is with you almost every step of the way, but won't hold your hand Orc by Orc.

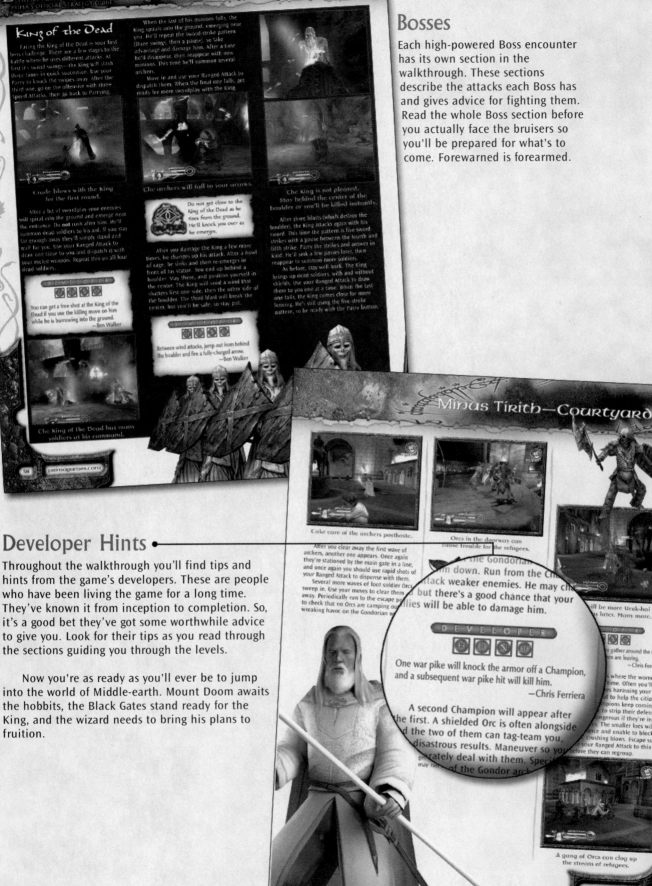

King of the Dead

Facing the King of the Dead is your first boss challenge. There are a few stages to the battle where he uses different attacks. At first it's sword swings—the King will slash three times in quick succession. Use your Parry to knock the swipes away. After the third one, go on the offensive with three Speed Attacks, then go back to Parrying.

Crude blows with the King for the first round.

After a bit of swordplay your enemies will spiral into the ground and emerge near the entrance. Do **not** rush after him. He'll summon dead soldiers to his aid. If you stay far enough away they'll simply stand and wait for you. Use your Ranged Attack to draw one close to you and dispatch it with your melee weapon. Repeat this on all four dead soldiers.

DEVELOPER

You can get a free shot at the King of the Dead if you use the killing move on him while he is burrowing into the ground.
—Ben Walker

The King of the Dead has many soldiers at his command.

When the last of his minions falls, the King spirals into the ground, emerging near you. He'll repeat the sword-strike pattern (three swings, then a pause), so take advantage and damage him. After a time he'll disappear. Then reappear with new minions. This time he'll summon several archers.

Move in and use your Ranged Attack to dispatch them. When the final one falls, get ready for more swordplay with the King.

The archers will fall to your arrows.

Do not get close to the King of the Dead as he rises from the ground. He'll knock you over as he emerges.

After you damage the King a few more times, he charges up his attack. After a howl of rage, he sinks and then re-emerges in front of his statue. You end up behind the center. Stay there, and position yourself in the center. The King will send a wind that shatters first one side, then the other side of the boulder. The third blast will break the center, but you'll be safe, so stay put.

DEVELOPER

Between wind attacks, jump out from behind the boulder and fire a fully-charged arrow.
—Ben Walker

The King is not pleased. Stay behind the center of the boulder or you'll be killed instantly.

After three blasts (which destroy the boulder), the King attacks again with his sword. This time the pattern is five sword strikes with a pause between the fourth and fifth strike. Parry the strikes and answer in kind. He'll sink a few passes later, then reappear to summon more soldiers.

As before, stay well back. The King brings up dead soldiers, with and without shields. Use your Ranged Attack to draw them to you one at a time. When the last one falls, the King comes close for more fencing. He's still using the five-stroke pattern, so be ready with the Parry button.

Developer Hints

Throughout the walkthrough you'll find tips and hints from the game's developers. These are people who have been living the game for a long time. They've known it from inception to completion. So, it's a good bet they've got some worthwhile advice to give you. Look for their tips as you read through the sections guiding you through the levels.

Now you're as ready as you'll ever be to jump into the world of Middle-earth. Mount Doom awaits the hobbits, the Black Gates stand ready for the King, and the wizard needs to bring his plans to fruition.

Bosses

Each high-powered Boss encounter has its own section in the walkthrough. These sections describe the attacks each Boss has and gives advice for fighting them. Read the whole Boss section before you actually face the bruisers so you'll be prepared for what's to come. Forewarned is forearmed.

Minas Tirith—Courtyard

Take care of the archers posthaste.

Orcs in the doorway can cause trouble for the refugees.

After you clear away the first wave of archers, another one appears. Once again they're stationed by the main gate in a line, and once again you should use rapid shots of your Ranged Attack to dispense with them.

Several more waves of foot soldier Orcs sweep in. Use your moves to clear them away. Periodically run to the escape po to check that no Orcs are camping ou wreaking havoc on the Gondorian w

...the Gondorian
...m down. Run from the Chi
...tack weaker enemies. He may ch
...but there's a good chance that your
...llies will be able to damage him.

DEVELOPER

One war pike will knock the armor off a Champion, and a subsequent war pike hit will kill him.
—Chris Ferriera

A second Champion will appear after the first. A shielded Orc is often alongside ...d the two of them can tag-team you, ...disastrous results. Maneuver so yo ...rately deal with them. Speci ...may ru... of the Gondor arch...

...ll be more Uruk-hai
...s later. Many more.

...to gather around the stairs
...em are leaving.
—Chris Ferriera

...s where the women
... time. Often you'll
...es harassing your
...t to help the citizens.
...pions keep coming.
...to strip their defenses.
...ngerous if they're in a
... The smaller locs will
...ance and unable to block
...crushing blows. Escape such
...e your Ranged Attack to thin
...before they can regroup.

A gang of Orcs can clog up the stream of refugees.

Gandalf

Gandalf knows that desperate plans are required as the specter of darkness grows over Middle-earth and Sauron's armies issue forth from Mordor to destroy the world of men. The white wizard helps liberate Rohan and the war is turned toward Minas Tirith, the last great stronghold of free people, where he intends to distract Sauron's gaze with a final, bold defense.

As an advisor of men, Gandalf musters the defenses of Gondor to stand firm in the face of darkness. As a warrior on the battlefield, Gandalf conjures shockwaves with his staff to knock enemies aside. Then with his sword, he slays them with ease. But victory cannot be won by force of arms alone, and Gandalf's plans are meant to buy time, knowing all hope rests in the success of Frodo's quest.

The wizard is one of the more effective characters in that he combines good speed with excellent damage, and has broad, sweeping attacks. Using his staff and sword in combination, Gandalf can tackle a large group of enemies with alacrity, striking them aside to avoid being overwhelmed.

The damage he does is considerable, as with most of the characters. This is important because an enemy that has been dispatched and not knocked down cannot bother you later on.

Gandalf's speed is a great asset. Due to the fact that he attacks with his sword and staff simultaneously, the wizard can deliver blows rapidly to the foes around him. He's faster than Aragorn and Gimli when using special moves. Thus he is less likely to be interrupted in the middle of an attack.

Another benefit of the two-weapon attack is that he is able to sweep at enemies who are crowded around him. As Gimli does with his axe swings, Gandalf makes broad motions when he strikes, which can hurt, or at least push away, the foes around him. Therefore, he's less vulnerable to getting mobbed and more able to escape a crush of opponents.

The wizard is a well-rounded character with many strong attributes and abilities. This is not surprising because his path is a solitary one. Unlike the other playable characters, Gandalf has no companions to help fend off hostile creatures during play. The wizard is alone but makes up for it with his speed, strength, and range of attack.

Aragorn

As the last descendant of the Kings of Men, Aragorn is fated to claim the long-empty throne of Gondor, should he prove worthy of this task. To fulfill his destiny, Aragorn must first pass through the Paths of the Dead and attempt to command the horrible foes who once betrayed Gondor. Then he must return to Minas Tirith and fight Sauron's horde in defense of this besieged city. And, should he survive this path, Aragorn must at last face the Dark Lord's servants before the very gates of Mordor.

As a ranger and Elf-friend, Aragorn's ability with the bow allows him to defeat opponents at long range. His true prowess, however, lies in close combat. Wielding a reforged Narsil, the legendary sword that defeated Sauron, Aragorn is a deadly combatant on the battlefield, easily defeating multiple foes.

Aragorn has a strong, deliberate attack. His speed is not the best, but his ability to cleave through foes balances that out. His heavy sword can make great sweeping cuts. In some of his upgrade moves, he strikes vertically with the final cut. This means he targets only one foe and doesn't push back or harm the enemies to either side. This can result in trouble with mobs. However, if Aragorn is caught in a crush of enemies his Speed Attack is sufficient to help him break away.

Aragorn's attack speed is not the best. He can be interrupted often while his special moves develop, aborting the motion and making him vulnerable to damage. To effectively battle with Aragorn, focus your energies on single targets. Instead of making random cuts to push the foes back, dispatch each enemy in turn to reduce the number of them crowding around you. Less creatures attacking you means you take less damage.

Aragorn's speed makes parrying that much more important. Being able to time the attacks of your enemies is a skill you'll develop as you play. Figure out what their patterns are so you can stop parrying, and attack when the time is right.

The son of Arathorn is a powerful character to play. His heavy attacks can help you carve through most enemies.

Legolas

Although the Fellowship that set forth from Rivendell has been divided, the friendship that binds these comrades together holds true. In support of Aragorn, Legolas and Gimli fight beside each other through hardship and peril, despite their differences. Yet their greatest challenges are yet to come, as they enter this war alone and are vastly outnumbered.

As a fighter, Legolas' skill with matched blades has won him the respect of his friends. But the bow of Legolas will often turn the tide of battle, as his deadly accuracy stops foes in their tracks. Legolas risks his own immortality in the cause of all free men, and he will not permit Aragorn or Gimli to go on without him—to whatever end.

The Elf's main characteristic is his speed. Fastest of the Fellowship, Legolas can rapidly strike an enemy. Combine that with the fact that he uses two blades, and the flurry of attacks he makes will keep a foe off-balance and interrupt most counterattacks.

This can lead to overconfidence. The Elf's whipping blades will knock down quite a few enemies in a short amount of time, but won't kill all of them. If you don't finish the combatant off with a Killing move, he'll get up to attack again. And it may not always be possible to use your Killing move in the heat of a battle.

Curb your enthusiasm when you play as Legolas and don't push forward too fast. If you move ahead to trigger future enemies while leaving a trail of stunned-but-not-dead foes behind you, you'll soon find yourself surrounded.

Beginning players will enjoy Legolas for his speed and the safety it can give you. His quickness makes him a forgiving character, letting you recover from mistakes faster. Keep a check on your pace and the Elf will see you through.

Gimli

As sturdy in spirit as he is in stature, Gimli the Dwarf is a formidable warrior. His skill with weapons and his unflappable spirit earn him a strong and unlikely bond with Aragorn and Legolas. Despite distrust between the Elf and Dwarf, all three of these warriors share a deep admiration for each other, forged in the fires of combat.

Armed with axes and sheer force of will, Gimli can quickly defeat enemies nearly twice his size. His ferocity in combat is a perfect compliment to the swordplay of Aragorn and the bow skill of Legolas. Together these companions intend to become an irresistible force, helping Gandalf turn the tide in their war against Sauron.

Due to his speed and size, Gimli needs precise handling when faced with the more crowded levels. However, he is capable of dealing out a good amount of damage. Plus, Gimli's attacks are suited to sweeping away several foes, giving him room to maneuver.

Do not think the Dwarf is a lesser character because of his smaller stature. There's just a steeper learning curve to mastering his play style than with his taller companions. His speed makes his attacks a little slower to develop, so be careful about your timing. Being short, he is easily lost in a crowd of enemies (especially in the Paths of the Dead), making it difficult to figure out which way he is facing. Keep him in clear sight, and use his axe to get him out of tight spots.

Gimli does best with a group of foes to his front, just waiting to be hewn with his war axe. The heavy blade will fell opponents like trees, or at least knock them back to give you room. Let Legolas wade in with Whirlwind Attacks while you concentrate on dispatching enemies to keep them from surrounding you.

Play deliberately with Gimli. Keep foes in front of you and move ahead at his

pace. You don't have to be as cautious as you might with a hobbit, but don't crash into huge waves of Orcs. If you get overwhelmed, pull back to a quieter space before moving forward again. Finish off enemies as you encounter them, but remember that in a pinch the Dwarf can handle a crowd with some of his upgrade moves and Speed Attacks.

Sam

Often the unlikely may become the great heroes, and Sam Gamgee is destined to become the greatest hero of all. Every step taken by a weary and worn Frodo brings these two hobbits closer to Mount Doom and the fulfillment of their quest. Sam is always at Frodo's side, his unswerving loyalty and conviction of heart giving them hope, despite the seeming impossibility of their task and the odds against their success.

Sam is a warrior created by necessity: determined, ferocious, and deadly despite his small size. His quick thinking and ability to use stealth to his advantage must get him—and Frodo—out of some very tight spots. Sam's greatest strength is his love for his friend and his commitment to seeing things through.

It has often been said that hobbits are slow to action but, once they get there, can forge ahead with a resolve and focus of purpose that belies their small size. Sam Gamgee typifies this description and no more so than in his activity during the game. Entrusted with the safety of Frodo, Sam will go to any lengths to see the Ring-bearer's quest fulfilled.

Playing as Sam can be satisfying. He moves well, has a good amount of speed, and a few tricks that make him fun to control. You won't have to deal with crowds of enemies attacking all at once, unlike the other Fellowship members, and it's just as well. Sam is suited to the type of combat he faces, usually a few enemies at a time, mostly in situations that allow you to deal with them in small bites.

There's still a chance that he can get mobbed (especially in Cirith Ungol), but if you tread with caution you'll be able to pick away at any crowd. Perhaps the single most useful move for Sam is Final Judgment. You gain it early on and it will serve you well throughout the game. The move lets Sam dispatch enemies with three button presses, saving him from toe-to-toe fights with larger enemies.

Sam's Ranged Attack will save him from facing enemies head-on. It's not something to rely on, because it's not as powerful as other Ranged Attacks. As a bonus, Sam can use his Elven Cloak to become invisible to his foes' gaze. While it slows him down to a walk, you can use the cloak in combination with your Killing move to perform a back-stab. Use the cloak (by pulling in the shoulder buttons) and sneak around behind your enemy. Then press your Killing move button and Sam will slay the creature.

Play Sam deliberately and with caution. He's a sturdy fellow, but wading into trouble isn't his style.

Basics

HEADS-UP DISPLAY (HUD)

To play *The Lord of the Rings: The Return of the King*, you'll have to understand the information presented to you on the screen as your adventure unfolds.

You need to pay attention to several meters as you play. Here's how they are laid out on your screen:

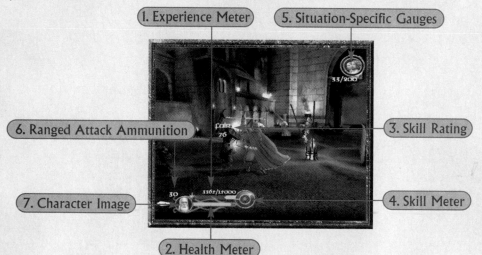

- 1. Experience Meter
- 5. Situation-Specific Gauges
- 6. Ranged Attack Ammunition
- 3. Skill Rating
- 7. Character Image
- 4. Skill Meter
- 2. Health Meter

1. Experience Meter

The blue bar shows a visual representation of how close (or far) you are from the next level. When it fills, you'll move up to the next level. You will also see a set of numbers above the bar. The number on the right is the amount of experience points you need to reach the next level; the number on the left is the amount of experience points you have. In the example shown in the screen, Gandalf has 3,365 experience points and he needs 15,000 to reach the next level.

2. Health Meter

The green bar denotes how much health your character has. When it's green, as in the screenshot, you're doing well. If the bar is drained below a certain point, it will turn yellow to warn you that your health is low. When it drains still lower, the bar turns a flashing red to indicate dangerously low health. Be on the lookout for healing health vials.

3. Skill Meter

The circular skill meter is a gauge of how well you're doing in combat. As it fills, you move up from Fair to Good, then Excellent, and finally Perfect. Each level awards you more experience points per enemy defeated.

 NOTE More details on experience, the Skill Meter, and skill levels are given later in this section of the guide.

4. Skill Rating

When you defeat a foe, a skill rating flashes onscreen with a number under it. The rating tells you where the Skill Meter is (in this example, it's only at Fair). The number below it lets you know how many experience points you've earned for the kill.

5. Situation-Specific Gauges

These gauges are not always in sight. If the situation calls for a new meter or counter, it will appear in your screen's upper right corner. There are cases where you'll see more than one gauge onscreen at a time. These gauges measure time, number of enemies you've killed, health of an ally, and so on. Whatever they measure, it's vital to the success or failure of your level, so pay close attention.

6. Ranged-Attack Ammunition

This number represents how many shots you have with your Ranged Attack. The maximum you can have is 30.

7. Character Image

This lets you know whose character information you're looking at. This may seem obvious during single-player gaming, but it can come in handy during cooperative play.

THE GAME LEVELS

When you start the game, you'll be shown the game's level tree. It's like a map of the levels that you'll be able to play as you progress.

There are three branches to the storyline: the Path of the Wizard, the Path of the King, and the Path of the Hobbits. Each one involves different members of the Fellowship. There are 13 levels total, broken down as shown in the table that follows.

 The playable characters listed here do not include the unlockable characters you can earn later in the game. Those will be covered in a separate section further on in this guide.

When you play a single-player game, you have to start at Helm's Deep. From there you can follow any of the paths. After completing a level, you can proceed to the next level on that path, but you must complete the lower level before moving on.

For example, you must successfully complete Paths of the Dead before moving on to The King of the Dead. You can, however, play the paths in any order you wish. You could play the Path of the Wizard from Helm's Deep to Minas Tirith—Courtyard before you start on the Path of the Hobbits. However, there is a storyline attached to this game, an epic storyline. To get it in the correct order, follow the path outlined in the walkthrough of this guide.

The three characters for the Path of the King.

The Path of the King must be played with all three characters: Aragorn, Legolas, and Gimli. This is because you won't be able to play the Black Gates level without first completing all the way up to (and including) the Pelennor Fields level with all three characters, *plus* you must complete the Path of the Wizard up to (and including) Minas Tirith—Courtyard. After that's done, you can play the Black Gates.

 The level map also holds some bonus material in the form of unlockable videos and slide shows. More details about that will follow in the Secrets section at the end of this guide.

CONTROLS

Since *The Lord of the Rings: The Return of the King* is a multi-platform game, your controls will vary depending on what game console you're using. Refer to your game manual for a breakdown of the various buttons. Our guide will refer to the buttons in generic terms, so you can use this book with any of the platforms.

Three things related to your controls merit special mention. One is crucial and the other two are often overlooked. These three bits of information are important to your success—fix them in your mind.

The Action Button

The floating ring will indicate that you can use your Action button.

Levels and Characters

Playable Characters:	The Path of the Wizard	The Path of the King	The Path of the Hobbits
	Gandalf	Aragorn, Legolas, Gimli	Sam
Levels:	Helm's Deep	Paths of the Dead	Escape from Osgiliath
	The Road to Isengard	The King of the Dead	Shelob's Lair
	Minas Tirith—Top of the Wall	The Southern Gate	Cirith Ungol
	Minas Tirith—Courtyard	ThePelennor Fields	The Crack of Doom
		The Black Gates	

Though mentioned elsewhere, the following is important enough to reiterate here: The Action button is essential. While you're playing through the levels, you'll find many things to interact with. Some are weapons (such as the war pikes), some are tools to help you progress (such as winches), but all will be helpful.

Look for the floating circle of Elvish writing. It indicates something you can interact with by using your Action button. Simply stand in or right next to the glowing circle and press the Action button.

Special Abilities

The character image shows how long you have until your special ability recharges.

Each character has a special ability that is activated with the shoulder buttons or triggers on your controller. For the non-hobbit characters, it's a boost that will temporarily increase the damage you do and make it easier to reach Perfect mode. Gandalf's ability calls forth a shield that protects him from damage and harms all enemies who come in contact with the glowing sphere. For the hobbits, it triggers the use of the Elven Cloak, which makes them invisible to enemies for a time.

The abilities are all temporary. The character image in the lower left of your screen will clock how long you have until the ability fails and how long it will take for the ability to recharge.

It can be easy to forget about the special abilities in the heat of battle. Don't. In the fiercest fighting, you need any edge you can get.

Back-Jump

While hard to picture in a static screen shot, the back-jump is perhaps the most overlooked ability in the game. With a quick press down on the direction pad of your controller, your character will leap backward. You can use this to avoid enemy strikes and to quickly retreat from a crush of opponents. Experiment with the back-jump to discover how useful it can be.

ITEMS

There aren't many items to find in *The Lord of the Rings: The Return of the King*, but you'll want to be familiar with what's available.

Red Health Vial

The red health vial restores a small amount of health. It's the most common health object, and is in fixed locations on some of the maps or may be dropped randomly by defeated enemies.

Green Health Vial

The green health vial is the strongest health restorative in the game. It may not fill your health bar, but it restores a large portion of it. You can find them in fixed locations in some of the levels or they may be dropped randomly by defeated enemies.

Ranged-Attack Ammunition

The Ranged-Attack Ammunition can be found in a few fixed locations on rare occasions, but mostly will be dropped by defeated enemies. They usually hold 20 rounds of ammunition for your Ranged Attack. The pick-up looks like a quiver of arrows, but it will restore any of the character's ranged ammo, no matter what weapon it is.

Elfstones

Elfstones are found throughout the game. They award you experience points whenever you pick them up. They are in out-of-the-way places, so explore each level carefully or study the maps provided in this guide.

GAINING EXPERIENCE

This is the screen where your experience points are tallied at the end of a level.

Why should you worry about experience points? Because you need to gain levels as you play so you can get stronger moves and other upgrades for your characters. (More information on that in a moment.) Here, now, is an explanation of the point system.

You gain experience as you battle through the game. The amount of experience you gain varies according to several factors. The type of foe you're facing and the level of your skill are both factors on how many points you'll earn for defeating an enemy.

The larger or stronger a foe is, the more points it is worth when you defeat it. A troll is worth more than a spider, for example.

The bigger they are, the more points they're worth.

The Skill Meter is a more complex concept. The meter is a circular gauge next to your health and experience bars, and fills up as you fight. The more impressive your moves are in battle, the more quickly the gauge fills. Not only that, but you must battle continuously to keep the gauge from draining. A pause in your activity will leach away the color from the Skill Meter.

 note Parrying can also fill up your Skill Meter.

As the meter fills up, you'll achieve different ratings. "Fair" is the first and lowest rating (when the meter is empty, you're at the "Fair" level). "Good" is next (when the meter is about one-third to two-thirds full, you're at the "Good" level). "Excellent" is the third level, starting where "Good" leaves off at two-thirds and lasting until the meter is all the way full. Once the meter is completely full, you'll reach Perfect mode.

Perfect mode is easy to spot. Your character will begin glowing.

When you hit Perfect mode, you'll be getting the maximum experience for each enemy you defeat, plus your attacks do extra damage. It lasts for a specific amount of time before you go to an empty Skill Meter.

Earn enough experience and you gain a level. The number of points needed to raise levels is the same for each character. For example, to get to Level 2 you need 3,000 experience points, no matter who you're playing.

Points per Level

LEVEL	EXPERIENCE POINTS NEEDED
2	5,000
3	10,000
4	25,000
5	40,000
6	55,000
7	70,000
8	85,000
9	115,000
10	145,000

 note You can gain levels higher than Level 10, but there are no more upgrades to purchase past the tenth level.

The totals shown in the table are cumulative. That is, you won't need to earn 5,000 points for Level 2, then start from scratch to earn a full 10,000 points for Level 3. You only have to earn 10,000 points total to reach the third level.

UPGRADES

The upgrade purchasing screen.

The upgrades are what boost your abilities and power in *The Lord of the Rings: The Return of the King*. As described earlier, you collect experience points as you play. At the end of each level you have a chance to use those points to purchase upgrades. So, as you might have guessed, more experience is better.

The upgrade prices, in experience points, are in two columns. The first shows the price of a move for the character you just finished using. The second column shows the price for that upgrade if you want to buy it for the entire Fellowship. You can only buy some things for a single character, and thus won't have a Fellowship price.

When purchasing an upgrade, always check to see if there is a Fellowship price. If there is, buy it for the whole group, not just the individual. The Fellowship price may be higher, but it's cheaper than buying the upgrade singly for each character.

While you can't share experience points amongst characters to raise their levels, you will be able to share experience points when buying upgrades. Let's say you finish a level with Gandalf and, after getting the upgrades available, you've got 3,000 experience points left. Then you finish a level with Sam. When you reach the upgrade screen, you'll be able to use all the experience you earned as Sam plus the 3,000 points left over from the Gandalf level to purchase upgrades.

The Upgrade Chart

Here you'll find a chart that includes all the upgrades for all the initially playable characters. The top row shows the generic term for the abilities. For example, the term "Ranged 2" refers to the first Ranged Attack upgrade available to the characters. The column under that heading shows the name of the upgrade by character. For Aragorn, Ranged 2 is called Dúnedain Arrows, but Gimli's Ranged 2 is called Erebor Axes.

The bottom section of the chart, below the character-specific names of the various abilities, you'll find the costs for each upgrade and at what level that upgrade is available to a character. For example, Ranged 3 will cost Gandalf 5,500 experience points and he can purchase it at Level 5. But for Sam, Ranged 3 will cost 7,000 experience points and he can't purchase it until he reaches Level 7.

Finally, the bottom row shows the cost for the upgrades if you buy for the whole Fellowship at once (when that option is available).

Upgrade Chart

CHARACTER	LINK 1	LINK 2	LINK 3	DEVASTATING 2	DEVASTATING 3	DEVASTATING 4	RANGED 2	RANGED 3	RANGED 4	RANGED 5	COMBO 1	COMBO 2	COMBO 3	COMBO 4	COMBO 5	COMBO 6	COMBO 7	COMBO 8
Aragorn	Orc Bane	Warrior Bane	Bane of Sauron	Ranger Fury	Wilderness Rage	Wrath of Númenor	Dúnedain Arrows	Rivendell Arrows	Mithril Arrows	N/A	Orc Hewer	Final Judgment	Balrog's Gambit	Dark Deliverance	Shield Cleaver	Lightning Strike	Helm's Hammer	Swift Justice
Legolas	Orc Bane	Warrior Bane	Bane of Sauron	Elven Fury	Elrond's Rage	N/A	Mirkwood Arrows	Lothlórien Arrows	Arrows of the Valar	Mithril Arrows	Orc Hewer	Final Judgment	Balrog's Gambit	Dark Deliverance	Shield Cleaver	Lightning Strike	Helm's Hammer	Swift Justice
Gimli	Orc Bane	Warrior Bane	Bane of Sauron	Dwarven Fury	Mountain Rage	Wrath of Moria	Erebor Axes	Moria Axes	N/A	N/A	Orc Hewer	Final Judgment	Balrog's Gambit	Dark Deliverance	Shield Cleaver	Lightning Strike	Helm's Hammer	Swift Justice
Gandalf	Orc Bane	Warrior Bane	Bane of Sauron	Fog of War	Wrath of Anor	Flame of Udûn	Light of the Pilgrim	Light of the Forges	Light of the Valar	N/A	Orc Hewer	Final Judgment	Balrog's Gambit	Dark Deliverance	Shield Cleaver	Lightning Strike	Helm's Hammer	Swift Justice
Sam/Frodo	Orc Bane	Warrior Bane	Bane of Sauron	Poison Blade	Cloud of Shadow	Cloud of Rage	Poison Daggers	Morgul Daggers	N/A	N/A	Orc Hewer	Final Judgment	Balrog's Gambit	Dark Deliverance	Shield Cleaver	Lightning Strike	Helm's Hammer	Swift Justice
Aragorn Cost	5,000	7,000	9,000	4,000	5,000	7,000	5,000	3,500	7,000	N/A	1,000	5,000	5,000	7,000	7,000	7,000	12,000	12,000
Aragorn Level	2	5	7	2	4	6	3	6	8	N/A	2	2	4	5	6	8	9	10
Legolas Cost	5,000	7,000	9,000	4,000	5,000	7,000	5,000	5,500	7,000	10,500	1,000	5,000	5,000	7,000	7,000	7,000	12,000	12,000
Legolas Level	2	5	7	4	8	N/A	2	5	7	9	2	2	4	5	6	8	9	10
Gimli Cost	5,000	7,000	9,000	4,000	5,000	7,000	5,000	5,500	N/A	N/A	1,000	5,000	5,000	7,000	7,000	7,000	12,000	12,000
Gimli Level	2	5	7	2	4	6	5	7	N/A	N/A	2	2	4	5	6	8	9	10
Gandalf Cost	5,000	7,000	9,000	4,000	5,000	7,000	5,000	5,500	7,000	N/A	1,000	5,000	5,000	7,000	7,000	7,000	12,000	12,000
Gandalf Level	2	5	7	2	4	6	3	5	10	N/A	2	2	4	5	6	8	9	10
Frodo Cost	5,000	7,000	9,000	4,000	5,000	7,000	5,500	7,000	N/A	N/A	1,000	5,000	5,000	7,000	7,000	7,000	12,000	12,000
Frodo Level	2	4	6	3	5	9	5	7	N/A	N/A	2	2	4	5	6	8	9	10
Sam Cost	5,000	7,000	9,000	4,000	5,000	7,000	5,500	7,000	N/A	N/A	1,000	5,000	5,000	7,000	7,000	7,000	12,000	12,000
Sam Level	2	4	6	3	5	9	5	7	N/A	N/A	2	2	4	5	6	8	9	10
Fellowship Cost	8,000	10,000	12,000	N/A	N/A	N/A	N/A	N/A	N/A	N/A	3000	8,000	8,000	11,000	11,000	11,000	20,000	20,000

CO-OP PLAY

Two human players against the forces of evil.

To finish *The Lord of the Rings: The Return of the King*, you'll have to play through with a friend. Selecting to play through in the co-op version means you have two active human players controlling characters at the same time. There are some things to keep in mind as you play, however.

Choose a Direction

Working at cross-purposes will get you nowhere.

When playing with another person, you have to coordinate your efforts. Since the camera needs to keep both of you in frame at the same time, you can't just shoot off in opposite directions. You'll get to the edge of the screen and not be able to make any more progress.

Make sure that you're moving in roughly the same direction. Getting caught up can be harmful.

Basics

Ability 1	Ability 2	Ability 3	Health 1	Health 2	Health 3	Health 4	Health 5	Damage 1	Perfect	Rising
Gondorian Sword Master	Kingmaker	N/A	Strength of Stone	Strength of Iron	Strength of the Fellowship	Strength of the Evenstar	N/A	Sword Mastery of Kings	Killing Zone	Rising Revenge
Light of Lothlórien	Galadriel's Gift	N/A	Strength of Stone	Strength of Iron	Strength of the Fellowship	N/A	N/A	Elven Bow Mastery	Killing Zone	Rising Revenge
Lonely Mountain Lore	Axe Mastery of Kings	N/A	Strength of Stone	Strength of Iron	Strength of the Fellowship	Strength of Gloin	Strength of Khazad-dûm	Dwarven Axe Mastery	Killing Zone	Rising Revenge
Wizard's Power	Power of the *Palantir*	Enchantment of the Heavens	Strength of Stone	Strength of Iron	Strength of the Fellowship	N/A	N/A	Power of the Istari	Killing Zone	Rising Revenge
Cloak of Haldir	Cloak of Celeborn	Cloak of Galadriel	Strength of Stone	Strength of Iron	Strength of the Fellowship	Halfling Strength	Baggins Strength	Strength of the Gaffer	Killing Zone	Rising Revenge
3,500	7,000	N/A	5,000	5,000	5,000	5,000	N/A	25,000	10,000	10,000
3	7	N/A	3	5	6	10	N/A	10	8	3
3,500	7,000	N/A	5,000	5,000	5,000	N/A	N/A	25,000	10,000	10,000
3	7	N/A	3	6	8	N/A	N/A	10	8	3
3,500	7,000	N/A	5,000	5,000	5,000	5,000	5,000	25,000	10,000	10,000
3	7	N/A	3	5	7	8	10	10	8	3
3,500	7,000	10,500	5,000	5,000	5,000	N/A	N/A	25,000	10,000	10,000
3	7	10	2	5	8	N/A	N/A	10	8	3
3,500	7,000	10,500	5,000	5,000	5,000	5,000	5,000	25,000	10,000	10,000
3	6	10	3	5	7	8	10	10	8	3
3,500	7,000	10,500	5,000	5,000	5,000	5,000	5,000	25,000	10,000	10,000
3	6	10	3	5	7	8	10	10	8	3
N/A	N/A	N/A	15,000	15,000	15,000	N/A	N/A	N/A	20,000	20,000

Share

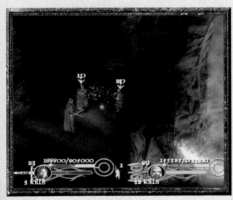

Health vials should be given to each according to his need.

There's a reason it's called cooperative play. It doesn't do you any good to be greedy. If your partner is in dire need of health, while your health is only slightly down, let them use the next health vial. Having a dead partner can only hurt your chances of getting through a level.

Likewise with other pick-up items, including Elfstones. Plus, don't try to hog all the battles. Sometimes it's hard to pick and choose your fights, but don't deliberately cut off your buddy from monsters so you can get the experience points. You want your partner to be on or near the same level as you so you can both be effective fighters in the later game levels.

Plan Upgrade Purchases

This is an addendum to the sharing rule. When it comes time to purchase upgrades and moves, Player 1 will have the first crack at it. If you are Player 1, do not go on a spree, spending points until there's nothing left. Player 2 has to draw from the same pool of points and needs to purchase upgrades, too.

Use the Upgrades Chart in this section of the guide to plan what you need to get. Buy Fellowship upgrades when possible and try to stay on even terms with each other.

It doesn't benefit you to be greedy. Share the points when it comes time to upgrade.

Combat

The Lord of the Rings: The Return of the King is full of battles and engagements with hostile creatures. You will have to fight continuously from one level to the next. However, don't think that a single-button-pressing, hack-and-slash approach is going to see you through.

The sheer volume of enemies, the sophistication of their blocking and attacking patterns, and the damage you can incur if you don't Parry all conspire to force you to learn how to fight wisely.

Staying alive is challenging.

THE BASICS

To begin your lesson, you must know that all playable characters have the same basic combat moves: Speed Attack, Fierce Attack, Ranged Attack, Parry, Kick, and Killing move. Plus, each character has an Action button he can use to perform various tasks, many of them related to combat. These form the building blocks for more elaborate moves, but for now take a look at each one in turn.

While each character has the same basic attacks (and they share a good deal of the upgrade moves as well), the strikes may not develop in the same way for each character. In other words, a move may look different, and in some cases act differently, from one character to the next.

Speed Attack

The simple Speed Attack is a quick horizontal strike with your character's main weapon. It can hit multiple enemies (if they're packed in close to your front) and moves you forward with each swing. You start out with a speed combo of three swings. Press your Speed Attack button three times to strike three times before pausing. This is useful for clearing away enemies that have crowded in or for keeping them off balance so they can't counterattack.

Fierce Attack

The Fierce Attack is a strong blow that can shatter an enemy's defenses (such as shields or armor). It's an underhand strike (except for the hobbits) that can knock over an undefended foe. You begin with a basic Fierce combo (press your Fierce Attack button twice) that makes your character strike two times, sending most enemies to the ground.

Ranged Attack

The Ranged Attack takes a couple of buttons to use, but use it you must. You'll need to hold a button down (usually a shoulder button) to bring up your range weapon, then press your Speed Attack button to fire. When enemies are inaccessible to Melee Attacks, you'll have to pull out the Ranged Attack to fight them from afar. To charge up a Ranged Attack shot, hold the shoulder button for a time before pressing the Speed Attack button to fire. As you play, you can increase the power of the

Ranged Attack with upgrades. These upgrades are character-specific: You can't do a Fellowship Upgrade for all Ranged Attacks.

Your character will automatically aim at an enemy when you bring up your ranged weapon. You can switch targets by moving the movement control. You cannot move your character while armed with a ranged weapon and the Ranged Attacks do not home in on your target. If the enemy is moving quickly across your field of view, you will most likely miss.

To charge up the Ranged Attack for a stronger shot, hold the Speed Attack button down for a moment. Your missile glows as it gains power. Release the button to let it fly.

Parry

The Parry button allows your character to block attacks. Parrying is vital to your survival. It's effective, thwarting all but the strongest blows. You have to keep tapping the Parry button to continue blocking, so press rapidly when surrounded by foes. You can't block troll attacks, so don't try—you'll end up hurt.

Kick

Use the Kick button to shove away enemies or special objects (such as ladders in the Minas Tirith—Top of the Wall level). More often than not the action your character performs is a shove, pushing at whatever is in front of him. When a foe is pushed he will stumble for a moment, allowing you to attack or slip by. This comes in handy when you need to escape a mob.

Killing Move

The Killing move is a finishing attack you can perform on enemies that are prone on the ground. It is lethal, no matter how little damage you've done to the creature beforehand. If he's lying on the ground, the Killing move will finish him off. However, it takes some time for your character to complete the finisher and you're vulnerable to attack while you do.

Action Button

The Action button isn't an attack by itself. However, it comes into play whenever you see a glowing white circle of Elvish words. The circle will be around things with which you can interact. Winches that lower ramps, war pikes to pick up and throw, grappling hooks for climbing, and siege weapons are all controlled by the Action button.

ENVIRONMENTAL WEAPONS

Use the Action button to interact with many objects in the game. While some of these help you progress along your path (such as winches to lower bridges), there are many objects for your use in battle.

War Pikes

The war pikes are found either stuck in the ground or heating up in a basket of hot coals. They are effective weapons. A single pike can take down a troll. A Champion enemy will fall after two war pikes (one to shatter his defenses, the second to slay him). As with Ranged Attacks, your character will automatically aim with the pike but you can shift it with the movement control.

The one drawback is that the war pikes take time to ready and throw. In that time, you are vulnerable to attack. If an enemy gets a hit on you before you launch the spear, it will clatter uselessly to the ground. Some braziers with war pikes will continuously regenerate the weapons; others are one shot only.

Brazier

These large metal basket-like holders contain hot coals and logs that will spill out in a rush when you tip them over. Wait for enemies to gather in front of a brazier, then push it over with the Action button. The fire won't kill them instantly, but wait a moment and they'll fall

Siege Weapons

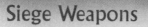

Siege weapons are on several levels. Ballistae (giant crossbows) and catapults are fixed in place. You can't aim them, you have to wait for something to walk in front of them, or fire them at whatever they're aimed. Some will reload for more shots, depending on the level.

Boiling Oil

In some levels, at points on fortified walls, are cauldrons of boiling oil. Use the Action button to dump them onto the field, and on any foes waiting there. The cauldron refills, allowing you to douse the area several times to ensure you've dealt with every enemy.

TACTICS

Taking the time to learn a few things about how to fight in the game world can save your character's health. Several tactics can maximize the damage you do while minimizing the risk to yourself.

When you look at it closely, the main point of survival in the game is "don't get hit." The less damage you take, the less likely you'll fall under the swords of your enemies. So the most important skill you can develop toward achieving that end is parrying.

Parrying techniques are offered here, then some general tactics to help you emerge victorious.

 For strategies that deal with specific enemy types, see the Monsters section in this guide.

Parrying

The Parry button makes blocking easy. Tap away at it while your enemies swing at you. Parry arrows also. Learning to parry is simple, but to make progress you need to know when to parry and when to stop.

Enemies attack with patterns. For example, Orcs have a lunging attack where they run at you, jump, and slice down. After that attack is over, they pause. Alternately, they take three swings at you with their swords in rapid succession, not unlike your basic speed combo. After those three strikes, they pause.

Combat

The running downstroke.

During their attacks you should be parrying. But after the attack is over, recognize that the enemy has paused and counterattack. As you play, you'll get used to the patterns and be able to quickly react. Use the lower levels as training grounds for this. Get to know your opponents so that when the fighting gets thick, you can deal with it.

The problems start when enemies mob you. A crush of enemies around you means that at any given moment, one of them is attacking. This leads us to the next tactic.

Crowd Control

Crowds are difficult.

Often you will be in battles where the enemies blanket the field. They'll smash into you and give you little room to maneuver. If you try a combo, you'll most likely get interrupted. There are a couple of ways you can deal with this.

The first is to hack away. This isn't always the best idea but if the crowd is not too thick, whip out a few Speed Attacks to knock down or slay a few opponents.

Another strategy is to use your Kick button to shove away the foes in front and use that opening to either attack or run.

Running is the third option, and not a bad one. If there is an opening in the throng (or if you create one with the Kick button), bolt. You will take hits as you go, but you can turn and fight, preferably after you get your back to a wall or other obstacle. It is important not to be surrounded. Having your enemies to your front is preferred so you don't have to worry about hits coming from all directions.

Putting your back to the wall is the best option when you're outnumbered.

Finishing Moves

If you have the advantage, don't waste it.

The Killing move may go unnoticed during a fierce fight, but don't forget about it. Taking a foe out quickly means one less sword raised against you. The fastest way to do that is with the Finishing move. Be careful because you are vulnerable to attack when using the Killing move, but using it judiciously can save wear and tear.

Consider your character's speed when using the move. Legolas is quick enough to pull off the attack in the middle of a crowd of hostile Orcs. Gimli, on the other hand, spends a long time spinning his axe before landing the final blow. Don't attempt the

finisher if you're surrounded, but remember it for those moments when you can dispatch an enemy with little risk.

Ranged to Melee

You can harm foes as they draw closer.

When facing enemies charging at you, ready your range weapon and fire off shots until they're within melee fighting distance. You can thin out a crowd or weaken an enemy before engaging in hand-to-hand combat. It will give you an edge and make the fight end sooner.

Allies

Your companions are a great help.

When playing solo, the non-player characters can help you survive. They aren't the best fighters (mostly they run interference), but they take some heat off you. Mostly you'll deal with computer-controlled allies in the Path of the King, with the two characters you aren't playing. However, they come in other forms as well. Gondorian soldiers, Frodo, and Rohirrim all make appearances as active allies in different levels.

When there are large battles and a number of allies to help (such as during the Pelennor Fields or Minas Tirith—Courtyard levels), shatter shields and armor of the enemies. You don't have to kill them, but taking away their defense leaves them open to your allies' attacks.

Your friends will often knock down a foe. So if you're nearby, use your Killing move to dispatch them.

You allies can sometimes save you from a crush of enemies. The Path of the King levels are prone to this. Your two companions will follow you and engage enemies around you.

UPGRADE RECOMMENDATIONS

There are plenty of moves and upgrades to choose from, and you'll be able to purchase most of them. However, there are some that you may want to get before others. Balance out the moves you purchase for the Fellowship, letting each character pay for one group upgrade. Making all of the Fellowship purchases with a single character will prevent him from getting character-specific moves that may be of great help to him later.

Here's a list of recommended purchases for the earlier levels.

Faramir's rangers and Gondor soldiers will also be of service.

Orc Hewer

This combo move is easy to use and effective. It not only deals a good amount of damage, it also knocks down your enemy. Used with characters such as Gimli and Gandalf, the Orc Hewer is a sweeping move that will affect several close enemies at once. Buy it for the whole Fellowship.

Strength of Stone

This upgrade increases your character's health, which means you'll be able to stay alive longer. Buy it for the whole Fellowship. There are several strength upgrades as you progress. Purchase them as they become available.

Final Judgment

Sam can use Final Judgment exclusively. The quick move ends in an instant kill, wiping out foes. Buy it for the whole Fellowship when it's available (which is immediately—it's a Level 2 upgrade). With just three button presses you can wipe out an opponent. This can save you from health-draining fights and thin out large crowds.

Ranged-Attack Upgrades

These upgrades are character-specific: You can't make a blanket purchase for the group. Pick them up with each character as you advance in levels. There are several, each one increasing the damage done by your Ranged Attacks.

Combat

CO-OP COMBAT

As mentioned in the Basics section of this guide, there's a hefty advantage to cooperative play.

The big difference with co-op is that you have two characters doing full damage and backing each other up. In single-player action, your allies are limited in their abilities and power.

Imagine the speed at which you can get through a level when there are two humans controlling fully active characters. Here are some ways to maximize that advantage.

Divide the Labor

One Ranged, one Melee makes for less damage to you.

In the more brutal encounters, designate one person to use Ranged Attacks while the other engages the enemy with Melee strikes. The Melee player can guard while the Ranged player slays or weakens enemies from a distance. When the Ranged player runs out of ammunition, the two of you should switch.

This is handy during levels like the Southern Gate. Make sure that the Melee player doesn't get too far ahead of the Ranged Attacker. Keep each other covered and you'll be a force to be reckoned with.

Back to Back

Play defensively in a mob.

When faced with an open area full of enemies, you can opt to go back to back in an attempt to keep yourselves healthy. Like dividing up the Ranged/Melee chores, this tactic requires cooperation.

Start by facing in opposite directions. You don't have to be pressed up against each other. The point is to cover your partner's back. Deal with the enemies to your front while your buddy does the same, and neither of you has to worry about enemies sneaking up behind.

Because your characters move forward as they attack you'll have to keep readjusting, backing up to stay in position and keep your friend safe.

Re-spawning

A fallen comrade can come back to fight another day.

You'll notice that your health bar displays have a silhouette of a figure and a number above it. This is the number of re-spawns you have between the two of you. Should one of you succumb to the attacks of your enemies, you will, after a time, re-spawn to

rejoin the fight. Watch the re-spawn counter. When it reaches zero, hit your Speed Attack button to come back to the fray.

You only get a limited number of re-spawns, so don't rely on them to see you through a level.

If one player is seriously hurt, let the other take the brunt of the action until you find health vials to tend to the wounds.

Ganging Up

Two on one is perfectly fair in a Boss battle.

When you come up against the Bosses during co-op play, you'll notice that they can't always focus on both of you at the same time. This is a decided advantage. Whether you're dealing with minions or the big Boss, having two people involved makes things easier.

Specifically, you can split the creature's attention. The Boss is only able to attack one of you at a time. Whoever's on the receiving end should Parry to stay safe while his partner is attacking.

This tactic also works well against regular enemies such as Champions. Be aware, however, that if your target gets in a good sweeping attack, it can get both of you. Practice your ganging-up skills on lesser creatures so you're ready when it's time to tackle bigger enemies.

29

Enemies

The forces ranged against you appear in several forms, from Orcs to ghosts. Within those forms are similar combat types, from Melee to Ranged. The combat types have various strengths and should be approached in specific ways. The tactics you use against them, no matter what their strengths, are the same.

The combat types are as follows:

- **MELEE: SWORDS, MACE, OTHER HAND WEAPONS**
- **SHIELDED: PROTECTIVE SHIELD PLUS POLE ARM**
- **RANGED: ARCHERS WITH BOWS OR CROSSBOWS**
- **CHAMPION: STRONGEST TYPE, OFTEN ARMORED**

COMBAT TYPE TACTICS

Whether you're dealing with a shielded Orc or a shielded dead soldiers, you'll use the same tactics. So here is some guidance on what those tactics should be. Later in this section you'll learn to look out for the different forms your enemies will take.

Melee Enemies

The melee enemies come at you with hand weapons and no other defenses. Their only option is toe-to-toe battle with you, so they begin with a rush and swipe of their weapon. You can see them coming as they run at you. Use your Parry to deflect their blows before counterattacking. Trying to meet their attack with a counterattack will end up with you getting hurt.

If the melee foe is close by, you can expect either Combo or Fierce Attacks. When they swing, expect them to make three strikes before pausing. Parry until the blows stop, then riposte. If you're surrounded by melee attackers, you'll need to time it so that you're attacking while all of your opponents are paused. This may not always be possible, but get in your hits while most of them are paused.

Shielded Enemies

The foes with shields can pose a challenge. They wield defensive shields that block any and all of your Speed Attacks. To get past this defense, shatter the shield with a Fierce Attack. After it's gone, you can do damage to the opponent with any attack you choose.

The shielded foes usually have a pole arm or other weapon with a long reach, in addition to the shield. These long weapons are a nuisance even after the shield is broken. Their reach can keep you at bay, unable to reach the enemy with your melee weapon. Parry their blows, then dart in to attack.

When you're in a crowd of enemies and some are shielded, you need to break their defenses before anything else. Use Fierce Attacks and direct them at the shielded foes. If you try to Speed Attack your way out, there's a good chance you'll batter uselessly at the shield.

Enemies

Ranged Enemies

The archers are armed with either bows or crossbows. Either way, they can attack from a distance. This can be deadly if you're swamped by enemies. While you're pinned down by melee types, the archers can pick away at you.

You can Parry their shots, but if there are six sword-wielding Orcs around you and four archers firing at you, it can get hectic. When you get a chance to deal with the archer, you can use your own Ranged Attack. Pause to bat away the archer's arrows, then fire once or twice, depending on how fast the archer's shots are coming. Pick away at the archer, shooting when you can, and parrying until the archer falls.

You can also attack archers head-on. The thing to remember is that the arrows do not track you as you move. If you're traveling at an angle to the archer (any way but straight at them), the archer's shots will miss you. Zigzag up to an archer if you attack head-on, or spiral toward one. Either way, be constantly moving as you approach.

Champion Enemies

The Champions are larger examples of enemy forces. Think of them as mini-Bosses. Wielding a weapon in each hand, they can do significant damage to you. Most of them (except for the dead soldier Champions) have armor that blocks your Speed Attacks. To get past it, use several Fierce Attacks to knock off the armor. You'll see pieces of armor fly as you hit them. Use a few to be sure they're undefended, then you can utilize any attack to bring them down.

> **note**
> Champions are recognizable by the health bar floating over their heads.

Use Combo moves on the Champions. The Rapid moves will keep the enemy off balance and prevent counterattacks. Keep the pressure on them until they fall. Many times a defeated Champion will drop a health object, so get the Champion out of the way.

ITEM DROPS

When you're in dire need, slain enemies drop items for you to pick up. They may disgorge red or green health vials or Ranged Attack ammunition.

More often, the Champions will drop items when defeated.

EVIL MINIONS

It's important to know what dangers lie in wait for you as you adventure through Middle-earth.

The enemy groups differ in strength as you progress through the game. The tactics discussed earlier in this section and in the Combat section of this guide apply to all the foes you'll meet. No matter their strength, use the advice against your opponents and you can win. In this part of the guide are examples of what you'll be up against.

Orcs

- **MELEE**
- **SHIELDED**
- **RANGED**
- **CHAMPION**

Bred as a twisted mockery of Elves, Sauron's Orcs lurk almost everywhere in Middle-earth where evil has gained a foothold. They are fairly weak and cowardly warriors, but are dangerous in sufficient numbers or against weak adversaries.

Saruman's Uruk-hai

- **MELEE**
- **SHIELDED**
- **RANGED**
- **CHAMPION**

Beneath Orthanc, the corrupted white wizard Saruman bred his own warrior army, perfected Uruk-hai soldiers, without fear. Equipped with the best weaponry his cunning mind could mass-produce from his forges—whose fires were fed by the trees of Fangorn—Saruman unleashed his hordes upon the unsuspecting people of Rohan.

Mordor Uruk-Hai

- **MELEE**
- **SHIELDED**
- **RANGED**
- **CHAMPION**

There are other Uruk-hai within the borders of Mordor, equally vicious and deadly. These Mordor Uruk-hai are often equipped with worn and scavenged armor and arms, but don't let their irregular appearance fool you: In battle they are deadly enemies! These warriors are the shock troops Sauron plans to unleash upon the walls of Minas Tirith. They are also used to bolster the guard of critical border forts such as Cirith Ungol.

Army of the Dead

- **MELEE**
- **SHIELDED**
- **RANGED**
- **CHAMPION**

The Men of the Mountain swore allegiance to Isildur thousands of years ago, but betrayed the Men of the West at the Battle of the Last Alliance. For their disloyalty, Isildur cursed them, trapping these ancient warriors along their ancient underground passages known as the Paths of the Dead. Within this haunted mountain, their specters still hover, animating ancient bones and awaiting liberation from their terrible fate.

Easterlings

- **MELEE**
- **SHIELDED**
- **CHAMPION**

The Men of the East have long been the enemy of Gondor, and they have sent formations of their warriors to the Black Gates in support of Sauron.

Haradrim

- **RANGED**

The deserts south of Gondor are home to this ferocious race of warriors. They have joined the war on the side of Sauron, bringing with them **mûmakil,** towering war beasts that can easily crush man or horse alike. Most of their troops ride atop these huge creatures, unleashing volleys of arrows in all directions. It is rumored that they carry a substance akin to Saruman's blasting powder on their backs, perhaps to assist in the destruction of Minas Tirith's walls.

The Haradrim are a special case in that they are only encountered while perched atop a Mûmak. Therefore, you can't rush them. You can only destroy the Mûmak's platform (using Ranged Attacks or handy siege weapons) to rid yourself of them.

Shelob's Children

The winding, cobweb-infested labyrinth of Shelob's Lair contains thousands of dead and dying life forms, trapped in webs and awaiting the arrival of Shelob's insatiable appetite. These tunnels also abound with smaller forms of spider life, perhaps spawned by the huge ancient creature herself, or perhaps merely using her lair to grow fat and bloated on her victims.

These spiders are a special case. The small spiders gather in groups that block your path. You can use nearby torches to temporarily disperse them. You can attack the larger spiders with regular weapons, but the Final Judgment move is the best move for dealing with them.

Monsters

Several creatures are beyond the bounds of the Melee, Shielded, and Ranged types. These beings require special attention if you are to defeat them.

Trolls

Trolls are huge beasts with enormous clubs. They can be disastrous if left to wander a battlefield. You need to quickly deal with them. The best option is a war pike. A single war pike can slay a troll. Make sure you aim properly—and let fly.

Failing that, use your Ranged Attack. Charge it up if you have the leisure. If you're pressed for time, shoot rapidly until the monster falls.

Fell Beast

The Fell Beast is the flying mount of the Nazgûl. When Fell Beasts appear in the air, use Ranged Attacks to damage them. As with the trolls, charge up your shots before firing. It may take several rounds to defeat the creature, but you can at least temporarily drive it off.

Mûmakil

Mûmakil are huge animals fitted with war platforms from which the Haradrim archers fire at their opponents. Being under the feet of a Mûmak is not advised: It will crush all those underfoot. There are shields alongside of the war platform. When charged with the task of dispatching a Mûmak, use war pikes, Ranged Attacks, or nearby ballistae. The pikes and ballistae will shatter a bank of shields in one blow. Ranged Attacks take a bit more. When the shields are destroyed, you'll see containers of blasting powder on the platform. Aim at them and fire until they explode, slaying the Mûmak in the process.

ENEMY BOSSES

The strongest of your foes, the Bosses require special tactics, discussed in detail in the walkthrough. When you come to the point where you encounter a Boss, the guide tells you what to do to defeat that Boss.

There will be several Bosses as you progress through the levels, and each one needs special handling.

Helm's Deep

Hornburg

Deeping wall

3

2 4

5

start

1

causeway

Helm's Deep

The Path of the Wizard

Character: Gandalf
Enemies: Uruk-hai, shielded Uruk-hai, archer Uruk-hai

THE FIELD OF BATTLE

Gandalf arrives with the riders of Rohan, not a moment too soon.

As the battle rages at Helm's Deep, Aragorn and his companions fight bravely against an overwhelming army. As promised, Gandalf arrives with reinforcements and engages the enemy forces. You will take control as soon as the Wizard engages the Uruk-hai.

This is a tutorial level, so keep your ears open for hints from the other characters. Watch the upper right corner of the screen for guidance on which button to press.

The first task is to defeat the four Uruk-hai facing you.

You'll immediately be up against a quartet of foes. Use the Speed Attack button to cleave through them. Do not forget to Parry—survival depends on your ability to defend against blows. Helm's Deep is the perfect place to hone those skills, so use the time wisely. This battle-field swarms with enemies.

After a few Uruk-hai fall, Legolas calls for help on the wall. Gimli points out the ladder leading to the Elf's position and climbs up.

The wall is charged and Legolas needs your help.

Before you arrive, you'll deal with Uruk-hai wielding shields. Use the Fierce Attack to shatter shields, then damage the soft parts underneath. Fight your way to the ladder and dispatch the foe at the bottom. Press against the ladder to start climbing to the top.

This Uruk-hai blocking your access to the ladder. Use your Fierce Attack to get by him.

Legolas and Gimli can hold their own on the wall until you get there. Build up experience points by battling on the ground a while. This can give you a boost in later levels.

Clear out areas to maximize your experience points.
—Mike Hurst

On the walls, flaming arrows from Orc archers pepper you. Parry to knock missiles out of the way, then use your Ranged Attack to fire at the archers. The battle won't last long after you attack, but it offers you experience with Ranged Attacks.

Batting away arrows is as easy as hitting your Parry button. Respond with shots of your own.

Soon Aragorn urgently summons you to save the causeway bridge. Looks like the Uruk-hai have to blow up the main gate. Legolas shows you the way, sliding down the rope of a grappling hook to the battlefield.

Before you follow him, deal with the host of Uruk-hai charging across the wall. Use your Ranged Attack until they get too close.

Aragorn has an important task for Gandalf.

Swat them away, get to the grappling hook, and press the Action button. Gandalf will climb down the rope to the field. Many Uruk-hai and men are locked in battle around a trio of ballistae (large crossbows). Ignore the Uruk-hai and go for the siege engines. Or, fight an Uruk-hai or two using spears from the cluster.

Using Ranged Attack while in Perfect Mode earns you big experience points. —Mike Hurst

Use a spear to dispatch a few enemies.

Don't take too long—the cart is making its way toward the main gate. Get to one of the ballistae and press the Action button. The weapon will fire, but won't quite stop the cart's progress. You'll need to fire all three ballistae to succeed. Fight off any meddlesome Uruk-hai and move from one siege weapon to the other, firing each in turn.

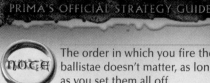

 NOTE The order in which you fire the ballistae doesn't matter, as long as you set them all off.

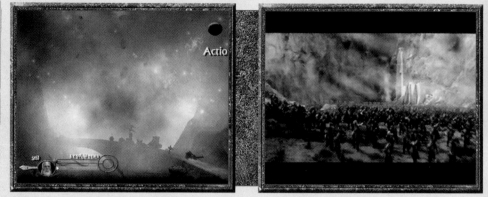 **TIP** If you have confidence in your combat abilities, spend time here fighting Orcs to build up experience points. Watch your health. If you fail the level here, you'll have to play the whole thing over. Take too long, and the level will end without you firing the siege bows.

When you set off the third one, it strikes the cart, causing a huge explosion and ruining the enemy's chance of taking Helm's Deep. Victory is yours in this battle, but how will you fare in the rest of the war?

The large crossbows will devastate siege engines. You need to fire off all three.

The cart is destroyed, the enemy routed, and Helm's Deep is saved.

Paths of the Dead

The Path of the King

Characters: Aragorn, Legolas, Gimli
Enemies: Army of the Dead, shielded dead soldier, archer dead soldier, dead soldier Champions

ALONG THE PATH

Aragorn and his companions must travel the Paths of the Dead in Dunharrow, a feared place populated by a cursed army's restless ghosts.

The need is great and the companions must succeed. The fate of Middle-earth may hang on their actions.

No matter which of the three companions you choose to play, the sequence of events and battles will be the same. Aragorn's heavy hitting style is a comfort amidst the restless dead you'll encounter. The Elf's speed may tempt you for your first run-through. Play through with all three, but for the first attempt Aragorn is a good choice.

Aragorn's heavy sword and medium speed is a strong combination as you enter the Paths of the Dead.

Run forward and you'll hear some choice comments from Gimli. A foggy mist cloaks the characters up to their knees (chest on the Dwarf), and slows your progress. Forge ahead to see spirits flying overhead. As you exit the fog, Aragorn warns that spirits can animate the bones around you.

mist fall
ROOM

crank
bridge

Checkpoint

spirit ROOM

start

column
ROOM

statue   gate

Paths of the Dead
Inbound

No sooner said than done, several dead soldiers appear from an alcove. Do battle as best you can. Block and strike when the creatures pause in their attacks. After you defeat them, a health vial appears in the alcove, if you need it.

Run along a couple of curves in the path to encounter more spirits ahead. At first they won't bother you, but as you proceed, a bone wall lurches out of the ground to block your way. Several dead soldiers emerge from the rock. You must destroy them before the way will open again.

If you're playing solo, this is a good chance to test the benefits and limitations of your NPC companions. Use your friends to block for you and get used to working with them. Use spears stuck in the ground, but only if the dead soldiers tangle with your friends. If you attempt to use a spear while an enemy is engaging you, you'll take a hit and lose the spear.

Waves of dead soldiers
will meet you here.

Don't stand too close to the bone walls or alcoves when enemies spawn, or you'll get knocked on the ground and sustain damage. —Paul Pettross

Your Fellowship companions will help
keep the crowd at bay.

Beware of threats in the fog.

When the last dead soldier is broken apart, the stone shatters, clearing the way. Another patch of fog slows things down. Gimli doesn't like the look of things. His instincts prove correct when a pair of caskets show up, disgorging a couple of dead soldiers. Deal with them and press on.

Ahead is a stone bridge where a pair of archer dead soldiers appear. Use Ranged Attacks to deal with them (pausing to block their arrows) or duck to your left. A ramp leads up, where you'll find another set of enemies. Make certain you're out of range of the archers and destroy the foot soldiers.

When that's done, continue up the ramp and deal with the archers (if you haven't already). Your companions will help out, knocking the archers off balance so you can get close to them.

After you're close to the archers, they easily fall.

Past the archers, you'll see one path leading ahead and one to your left. Move ahead, into the arms of a pair of dead soldiers. Destroy them and press on. An outcrop is found to the left, past a row of bone piles. Pick up the Elfstone at the edge and get ready as the bone piles immediately animate with spirits. Several dead soldiers attack. Carve your way through them and continue on the path.

The path ends at another outcrop. This one balances a boulder on its edge. Step up to it and use the Action button. Your character will drop the boulder on the dead soldiers milling below. Backtrack to the turnoff, past the first set of archers.

Pick up the Elfstone, then fight to the path.

Drop the boulder on the unsuspecting dead soldiers to make your journey easier.

There's a red health vial down a path to your right. Grab it if you need it, then get on the main path. You'll encounter a pair of shielded dead soldiers. You need to use a Fierce Attack to break their shields before you can damage them with Normal Attacks.

The shielded foes require more force.

You've passed that challenge and now you find the shielded dead soldiers who remain after the boulder drop. Use Fierce Attacks to get through their defense, then disperse their bones.

A few curves in the path and one encounter with dead soldiers, and you'll come to a gorge with a raised drawbridge. There's a winch to one side, in full view of the three archer dead soldiers on the other side of the gorge. Stand in front of the winch and use the Action button to turn it, lowering the bridge. Three turns will get the bridge down, but if you wait too long between presses of the Action button, the bridge will raise again.

Use the Action button to activate the winch and lower the bridge. The archers will attempt to thwart you.

 Use the health vial near the base of the bridge if you need it.

The best tactic is to stand near the winch, wait for the archers to fire so you can block their arrows, then press the Action button. You should have enough time to get in three turns before they fire again. (You may take a hit on the third try, but it's worth it.) When the bridge is down, run across to reach a **Checkpoint**.

FARTHER ALONG THE PATH

Across the drawbridge is a foggy area, slowing you. The specters are circling. As you wade into the mist, caskets crash through the floor, surrounding you and depositing more dead soldiers in your path.

The fighting is thick, so keep your companions near to absorb blows. Work your way through the enemies nearby, then go after the archers on the ramp against the wall. Dispatch them and the archers at the ramp's top. Pick up a red health vial at the top. Then go into the fog and continue.

It's a trap, but you'll be able to fight through it.

The next area is full of columns that will fall to make a switchback path to follow. It's also full of different types of dead soldiers. If you're playing solo, don't rush ahead of your companions. Make sure they stay near to occupy foes. Take your time, using your Block and Fierce Attacks to keep yourself healthy.

Friends can help take the pressure off.

Beyond the switchbacks is another patch of fog, but nothing lurks within it. Beyond is a ladder set in the wall, guarded by dead soldiers. Fight them off and climb up. Another bone wall rises to block your way and spawns a group of ghostly enemies.

After hacking through a few regular dead soldiers, you're faced with a stronger dead soldier who wields two swords. You'll notice him by the health bar above his head. Attack quickly to bring that energy down and shatter his animated corpse. After he's down, the way clears. Press on.

This strong dead soldier can take a lot of damage. Attack quickly to keep him off balance.

Farther along the path is an alcove to your left with a red health vial. Grab it if you need it. Beyond is a large room with a giant statue. Move closer and a rank of dead soldiers attack. Clear them away, then stand before the statue and press the Action button.

The statue topples, creating a bridge to a closed gate across a gorge. Cross to the gate and follow the path to the left, which winds under the statue/bridge and up to a winch.

A pair of dual-sword-wielding spirits attack. Scatter them, and their alcove reveals a health vial. After they're gone, concentrate on the winch, using the Action button to raise the gate.

Don't bother with the winch until after you win the battle.

On your way back under the statue/bridge, more shielded dead soldiers show up. Luckily they don't swarm, so you can deal with them singly. After that's done, head out through the gate.

A little farther, and the path opens into a huge chamber. Legolas states it is where the dead gather, an evil place. The only way out is across a narrow bridge. Start across and two rocks jut out of the bridge, blocking you at either end, and dead soldiers pour out.

This engagement will be taxing. It will take all your skill to get through.

Notice the counter in the upper right corner of your screen. You must defeat the number of enemies shown before you can proceed. As you fight, the foe type will change, from common dead soldiers to ones with shields, archers, and dead soldier Champions. When you've fought off the amount shown on your HUD, the rock blocking your way breaks apart. Get across the rest of the bridge and out of there. You've successfully completed the Paths of the Dead.

Road to Isengard

The Path of the Wizard

Character: Gandalf
Enemies: Uruk-hai, shielded Uruk-hai, archer Uruk-hai, Orcs, archer Orcs

THE FOREST PATH

It's time to address the issue of Saruman's treachery. He's turned Isengard into a fortress, raised an Uruk-hai army, and destroyed trees, which has angered the Ents. Gandalf is there to support the massive creatures in their fight. Chase the Orcs running away down the forest paths.

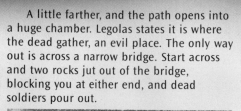

They may be running, but the Orcs have some fight left.

A few creatures come at you. Parry their large swords then answer their attacks with a few of your own. As you near a tree fallen across the path, you'll see an Ent tromping through the forest. Gandalf urges it on to Isengard, crying out that he will deal with the Orcs in the forest.

Your first encounters are warmups for what is to come.

Just beyond, you'll face Uruk-hai on the ground and an archer in a rotted tree above the path. Fight the two ground soldiers under the tree and avoid the arrows. When they fall, back up and use your Ranged Attack to destroy the archer Orc.

Now you'll see a cart piled with explosive charges. Wait for an enemy to draw near, then fire your Ranged Attack to blow it up. You must still deal with an archer on the hill. Use another shot to destroy him.

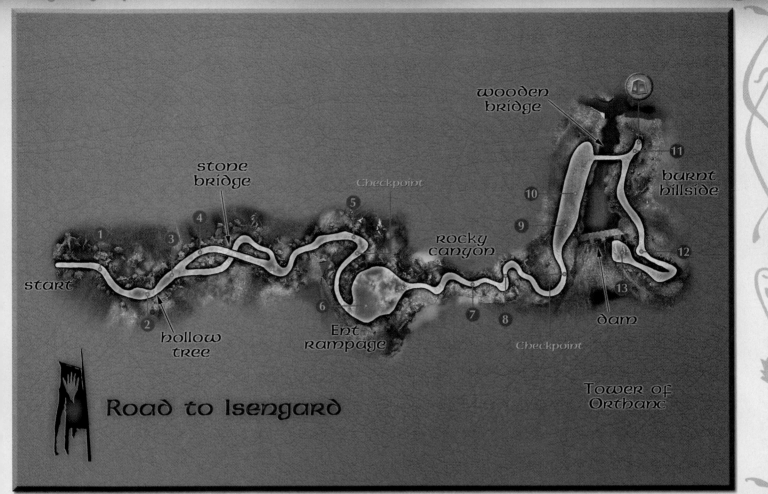

stone
bridge

wooden
bridge

Checkpoint

burnt
hillside

Rocky
canyon

start

hollow
tree

Ent
Rampage

dam

Checkpoint

Tower of
Orthanc

Road to Isengard

The Orc in the tree is an archer,
and won't take much to defeat.

The cart will do some of the
work for you, but don't ignore
the archer on the hill.

The path splits after the cart encounter. To the left is a stone bridge. At the foot of the bridge is a cart full of explosives. Quite a few Orcs are gathered around it, and there are two archers at the peak of the bridge.

Use your Ranged Attack to set off the explosives, then use the same projectiles to deal with the archers. You may have to pause to Parry a few arrows as you work. You could then cross the bridge, but to gain experience points, head down the right fork instead. This leads you under the bridge, into the midst of another group of foes. Fight them off and continue on. You'll emerge at the opposite side of the bridge.

will charge. Do away with them, then decide: Wade into the fray and risk getting stomped (but collect a lot of experience points), or stay at the foot of the slope and use Ranged Attacks to pick off foes and let the Ents do most of the work.

DEVELOPER HINT

The Ent rampage area is an experience gold mine. Kill as many Orcs as possible.   —Michael Q. Lin

Being around angry Ents
is perilous work.

Orcs are gathered on the bridge and under it. Take the time to dispatch them all.

The hairpin turn is an ambush point. Be prepared to fight.

Press on and you'll encounter more foot soldiers. Near the hairpin turn, a pair of archers is hiding in the brush. Use your Ranged Attack to flush them out and continue on. Just at the turn, a gaggle of enemies will rush in to hamper your progress. Parrying is important. Do not get surrounded—keep them in front of you as you attack, blocking when they start swinging.

When it's clear, turn to your right and you'll hit a **Checkpoint**.

CHECKPOINT

THE ENTS

Down the narrow slope, the Ents are rampaging around a circular clearing, stomping and sweeping away all creatures in their path. You can't progress until a set number of Orcs have been defeated. The counter will appear in the upper right corner.

Any Orcs the Ents destroy count toward your total. This is good news, since the Ents will crush you if you get underfoot. Head to the bottom of the slope and a group of Orcs

Whichever you choose, after you reach the limit on Orcs, a path leading forward will open. Follow it. Through the rocky canyon, you'll encounter a few foot soldier Orcs (with archers to back them up) on an outcrop. Deal with the immediate threat first (the ground troops) then knock out the archers with your Ranged Attack. When the first few are defeated, another group of archers show up. Use the same attacks on them to clear the way, then press on.

The archers are well hidden in brambles but your Ranged Attack will still be effective.

A few more turns in the path and you'll find a large group of hostiles.

Continue down the rocky canyon and a crush of Orcs will come at you. Parry first, then use Speed Attacks to clear them away. If you have the Orc Hewer move, Gandalf can use it effectively against a group.

The Tower of Orthanc is in sight.

You'll get a quick look at the Tower of Orthanc as you move forward. Then you'll hit a **Checkpoint**. A few steps beyond that is another cart of explosives and more Orcs.

CHECKPOINT

A shot with your Ranged Attack takes care of your foes, allowing you access to the next level.

Aim for the cart and let fly.

Beyond the cart is a gorge with rickety towers on the other side. The Orcs have unwisely placed a cart of explosives at the base of each tower. You must set off the explosive carts under each. Beware: Each tower has a set of archers and all of them are firing at you. Parry their arrows (or dodge out of the way) as you make your way down the line, targeting and setting off the carts.

As you run along your side of the gorge, foot soldier Orcs will attack, distracting you from your tower destruction. Dispatch them and continue targeting carts.

DEVELOPER HINT

The first tower at the dam can be blown up from the trail in the area just before entering the riverbank.
—Michael Q. Lin

Swat away the arrows, then fire on the carts.

You'll see a bridge. Pass by it at first and destroy the last two towers. Once they're down, go back to the bridge and start to cross. A pair of shielded Uruk-hai will block the way. Use your Fierce Attack to smash their shields. Don't get impatient, use your Parry until you get the right opening or they'll take turns carving you up.

Once across, go left to find an Elfstone. More foes will rush you. Destroy them, then carry on down the path.

Luckily, they can't surround you at this point.

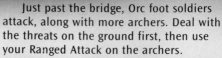

Just past the bridge, Orc foot soldiers attack, along with more archers. Deal with the threats on the ground first, then use your Ranged Attack on the archers.

After they're cleared away, head down a narrow path, which opens to a small plateau where another horde of Orcs awaits. An archer takes shots at you to keep you distracted. Take your time and Parry to keep safe.

This archer will fall easily to a Ranged Attack.

Keep to the path and you'll soon see an Ent attempting to break the dam that overlooks Isengard. Orcs are harrying it with flaming arrows. Your task is to keep the Orcs from bothering the Ent as it works on the dam.

Realize that there are archers on the other side of the dam, too. Clear out the area on your side, then use Ranged Attacks to get the ones across the way. A tough Uruk-hai Champion guards the two archers. To begin, focus all your energy on him until he falls, then knock down the two archers on your side and fire shots at the archers on the other side.

DEVELOPER HINT

The Orc champion at the bottom of the dam is easier to defeat if you hit him from a distance with a charged Ranged Attack.
—Michael Q. Lin

Several waves of Orcs will attack. Do not forget about the opposite side of the dam: Whenever you have a break in the action on your side, aim a few shots at the other platform to clear away any archers gathered there.

After dealing with the strong Uruk-hai, you'll be faced with several waves of Orcs. Don't ignore the other platform, or the Ents will never finish pulling down the dam.

Given enough time to work in peace, the Ents will yank the supports from the dam and send the river crashing into Isengard. The waters flood the plain, bringing an end to Saruman's plans.

Escape From Osgiliath

bath house

7 **8** Checkpoint

rooftop

balcony

up to rooftop

3

4

2

6

ladder down

start

5

1

collapsing tower

Osgiliath
map 1

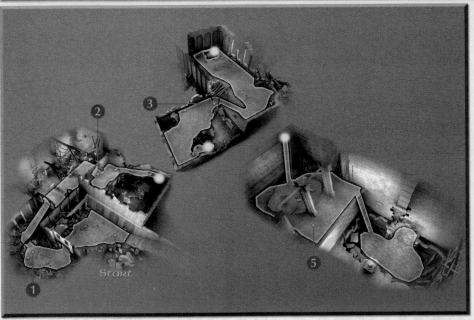

2 **3**

1 Start **5**

The Path of the Hobbits

Character: Sam
Enemies: Orcs, shielded Orcs, archer Orcs

TO THE BALCONY

The hobbits and Gollum must escape from Osgiliath as a fierce battle rages around them. Gollum leads the way but every turn seems to take you deeper into the fray.

Follow Gollum to the opening in the wall. Beyond you'll encounter the first Orcs in this level. Sam is not a powerhouse but he's a sturdy hobbit. Parry often, strike when there's an opening, and you'll get through.

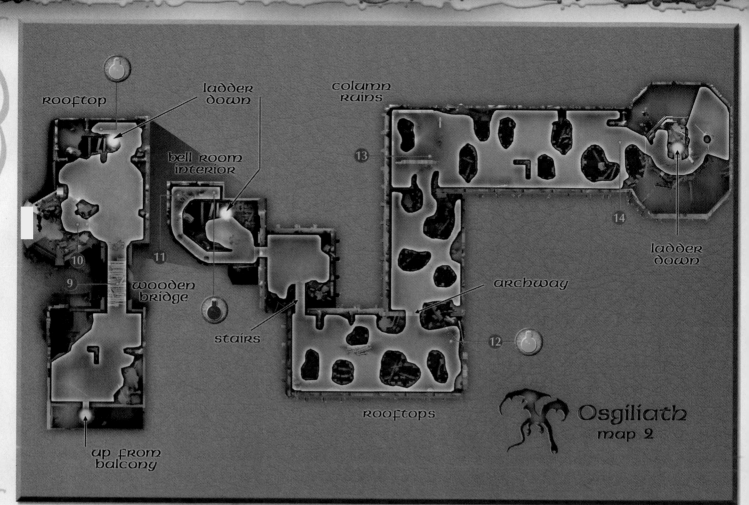

rooftop

ladder down

column ruins

13

bell room interior

14

10

ladder down

9

wooden bridge

archway

stairs

12

rooftops

Osgiliath
map 2

up from balcony

These are the first two Orcs
that Sam must deal with.

Past the hole, stairs appear with an
archer at the top. Use your Ranged Attack
to deal with him and climb the steps. Above
is a ruined walkway with a few Orcs that
will pay attention to you and a couple who
are fighting a man farther on. Deal with the
Orcs assigned to you, then move closer to

the next fray. Before you reach it, the wall
blows out, killing the combatants and
opening the way forward.

Orcs attack as an archer
takes shots from afar.

Past the hole, more Orc soldiers attack
you as an archer fires at you from across
the way. Take out the soldiers, then climb
up the ramp of rubble to the left. (You can
use a Ranged Attack to deal with the archer
if you feel the need.)

Once up on the rooftop, a Nazgûl
appears. The Ringwraith is riding its flying
mount, a Fell Beast, searching for the One
Ring. A meter appears in the upper right
corner. If the meter fills, the Ring has been
found and you'll fail the level. You must get
under cover to avoid the Nazgûl's gaze.

DEVELOPER
H I N T

Never let the Fell Beast timer fill up completely!
Seek shelter under rooftops and covered areas to
hide from the Fell Beast. Gollum may sometimes
point you toward out-of-the-way hiding spots.
—John "J.C." Calhoun

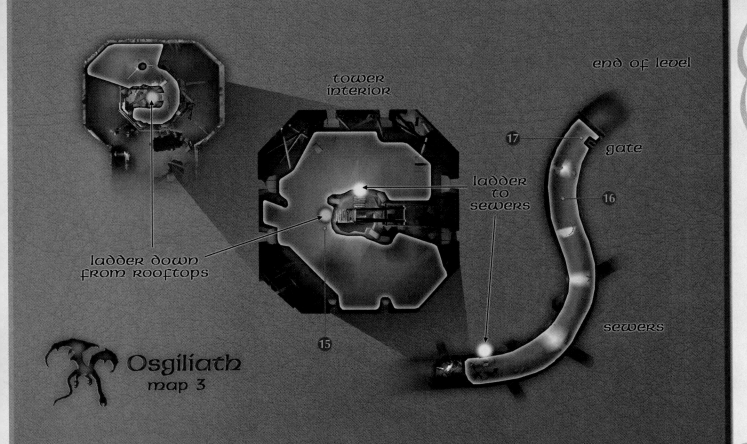

tower interior

end of level

ladder to sewers

17

gate

16

ladder down from rooftops

15

sewers

Osgiliath
map 3

The Ringwraith is searching for the Ring. You mustn't let him find it.

Before you reach cover, you must fight your way across the rooftop. Your first goal is a section of boards that will shield you from the Ringwraith. The going is easy. Men are fighting all the Orcs nearby, so head across the open area to the next corner.

 For a few extra experience points, destroy the Orcs the men are fighting. Keep an eye on the meter, however, and get under cover before it's full.

When you arrive, a pair of Orcs hops down the steps to battle you. Stay under cover and fight, and the Ringwraith meter will go down.

Fight these Orcs, but stay under the boards as you do.

 It doesn't matter if Frodo is under cover. Keep Sam out of sight and the Ringwraith meter will go down.

Up the stairs, a pair of archers have their backs to Sam, which makes it easy to cleave through them. Push on toward an open expanse of roof with a gaggle of Orcs waiting for you. A catapult shot crashes down upon them, leaving only two to deal with. Rush them so that you're under cover as you fight. There's a ladder leading down a hole. When the Orcs fall, climb down.

DEVELOPER HINT

Sam and Frodo are strong, but only against small groups of enemies. Try to lure Orcs closer to you, rather than running forward into a raging battle.
—John "J.C." Calhoun

It's a lucky thing that catapult shot landed where it did.

Being a hobbit allows you to sneak up on Orcs.

DEVELOPER HINT

If you use a physical attack on an enemy while he is near an edge, you can push him off for an easy victory. Try this near ledges, holes, and rooftops.
—John "J.C." Calhoun

Another pair of unsuspecting Orc archers is at the bottom of the ladder. Defeat them, then slide down the next ladder.

Past the bottom of the ladder is a wide-open area full of men and Orcs fighting each other. Sam is upset at Gollum for leading you here, but you'll have to wade through. It's not as bad as it seems. The men are keeping most of the Orcs busy and the Nazgûl can't see you down here. Take your time, parrying and fighting as you go. Don't rush or you become surrounded.

Fight slowly across this open area, even though Frodo wants you to go fast. You'll gain experience and keep from being swarmed.

If you're up to it after you defeat the rest of the foes, fight the Orcs engaged with the men. Either way, head for the steps on the opposite side, where you'll encounter an archer at the top. Pick up the red health vial beside the staircase if you need it.

The stairs are your goal. Grab the health vial before ascending.

Past the stairs is another room containing enemies. There are a couple of Orc soldiers and two archers on a rubble ramp. Deal with the soldiers. Use your Ranged Attack to take out the archers, or charge them. Once clear, climb the ramp to the next level.

The archers are nasty. Parry, then throw Sam's knives at them.

A few Orcs wait in the broken walk. Plus, the archer in the back is dangerous. Fight through the soldiers, then face off with the archer. Right near him is a green health vial.

After the way is clear, duck through the hole in the wall onto the balcony. It's a **Checkpoint** so you can breathe a little easier.

CHECKPOINT

If you're in need, fight through to the health boost. Or duck out the hole first to hit the *Checkpoint*.

UP TO THE ROOFTOPS

The battle is raging high and low.

After you hit the checkpoint, there is a ladder leading up. At this level you'll be exposed to the Ringwraith, so keep an eye on the meter in the screen's upper right corner. There's no time to dawdle; pass the Orcs and men locked in combat and only engage the foes that directly come at you.

DEVELOPER

Stay close to Faramir's Rangers for protection. Let them fight for you in tough situations.
—John "J.C." Calhoun

Head to the wooden bridge that links the two roofs. It's festooned with Orcs. You can engage them or dodge around them, depending on your Ringwraith meter. For the sake of experience, and to avoid any cheap shots, dispatch the bridge Orcs. A human archer at the top of the bridge helps you out, so it shouldn't take too long.

The bridge is a chokepoint. Either fight your way clear or run to the top.

When you reach the higher roof, move to your left and under the broken tower's cover. Orc archers appear, along with another soldier. Stay behind the pillar to escape the arrows as you deal with the soldier. Pop out to Parry away arrows and take down the bow-wielding Orcs.

Poke your head out the other opening of the tower and more Orcs attack. Deal with them, then stay under the tower until the Ringwraith meter is empty. When you're ready, continue down the ladder, battling any foes as you go. Grab the health potion if you need it. Use the ladder to go inside the buildings.

You have one soldier and three archers to take care of. Don't forget about the Nazgûl.

Snap up the health potion, then climb the ladder to escape the Ringwraith's gaze.

The ladder ends near a group of Orcs.

At the bottom of the ladder, Orcs attack you. Dispatch them, then turn to the staircase. Start up the bell room steps, but beware of enemies on their way down. There is a large bell at the top.

Stand behind it and use your Action button to shove it. The enormous metal bell tumbles down the steps (and over a few Orcs) to smash open a door blocked by rubble. That's the way forward. A red health vial is there for you on the landing, so grab it if you need to, then head down the staircase.

One push gets the bell moving. It's an impressive fall, ending with a spectacular crash.

Men of Gondor are fighting Orcs outside the bell room. Let them take the brunt of the blows, but take a moment to dispatch a few enemies.

Run upstairs to the rooftops. This long expanse is within the Ringwraith's sight, so the meter will appear again and bears watching. You'll find cover as you go, but foes will hamper you.

The Orcs will come at you on the roof. Go around or through them.

Don't panic as you move along the rooftops. The meter isn't fast, and you have time to battle and reach a safe spot. The first cover is opposite the stairs. You have to navigate through Orcs and men (fighting them if you want to) to get there. The first cover is a lean-to of boards in a corner with a green health vial underneath.

Reaching this structure shields you from the Ringwraith. Fight off the Orcs that attack.

The next area is reached by climbing a small pile of rubble. Dart to that area, destroy the nearest Orcs, then return to cover. Let the meter empty, then dart to the new area. This saves time when you run for the next cover. You may use the same tactic more than once to clear the way.

When you're ready, press on across the roof to the shattered remains of an archway. It may seem exposed, but it's your cover, so stay under it until the meter runs dry. Archers take shots at you, so stay on guard.

These two Orcs are between you and safety.

Clear out the area around the first ladder, then climb down the second ladder.

This brings you to the sewers of Osgiliath. Frodo insists you press on. Around the first bend, a band of Orcs charges you. Keep your head and you'll get through fine. You're almost out of the besieged city.

A lot of Orcs await you between safe points. Thin them out before moving on.

TO THE SEWERS

You're safe from the Ringwraith but the archers are still after you.

Once under cover, you'll be attacked by more Orcs. Archers pop out to fire on you. Fight, then climb down the ladder, or grab the ladder and climb down into the building.

Either way, at the bottom of the ladder Orc soldiers attack you. Cleave your way through them, then look at the ladder that leads down through a hole in the floor.

There's more fighting to be done in the sewers.

Around the next bend, things get tougher. There are a lot of archers and a tough Orc Champion with armor and two weapons. Use your Ranged Attack from afar to get the archers out of your hair before the big Orc comes after you. Health vials are available beyond the Orc group, but it's dangerous to rush after them.

Watch out for the archers. They can hit you while you're waiting for the meter to go down.

Consider forays out from under cover to deal with Orcs, then scuttle back. Your goal is a more intact tower. The problem is that an archer guards the front, and when you reach him, a pair of Orc soldiers leap out to block your way. You must fight them to get under cover, so make sure you save time on the meter.

If time is short, ignore the archer and concentrate on the soldiers. Get through them to the tower cover. Once there, be on guard: The fight's not over yet.

 If you need health, rush the group, then use your Elven Cloak and sneak past to the health vials. It's a risky ploy, but it might work.

DEVELOPER HINT

Did you know Sam can perform an "instant kill" while cloaked? Cloak yourself, then sneak behind an enemy and do a finishing move; Sam will perform a fatal back-stab. This is a great way to defeat the Orc commander in the sewers.   —John "J.C." Calhoun

If you're going to attack the large Orc head-on, you need to prepare. Lure him away from his fellows or use Ranged Attacks to dispatch them from afar. The big Orc has armor that will turn your attacks. You need to hit him several times with a Fierce Attack to knock away his protection. Parry his blows (he'll strike three times in quick succession with his sword, or once with his hammer), then employ a Fierce Attack. Repeat until the armor is gone. After he's vulnerable, use Speed Attacks to take him down.

This Orc may be big, but after his armor's gone you can win the fight.

When the Orc Champion falls, move forward to the gate he was guarding. You may find a few more Orcs to contend with. When the last of this band of foes has fallen, pick up the health vials at your leisure. Grab what you need, then face the winch. Press the Action button. Turn the winch three times and the gate opens.

There is sunlight on the other side. You are now that much closer to Mount Doom.

The winch operates the gate.

The King of the Dead

The Path of the King

Characters: Aragorn, Legolas, Gimli
Enemies: King of the Dead (Boss), Army of the Dead, shielded dead soldiers, archer dead soldiers

BATTLING THE KING OF THE DEAD

Sealed off from the others, you'll need to face the King of the Dead alone.

The request to join the Armies of Men is summarily rejected. The King is not in the mood for talk.

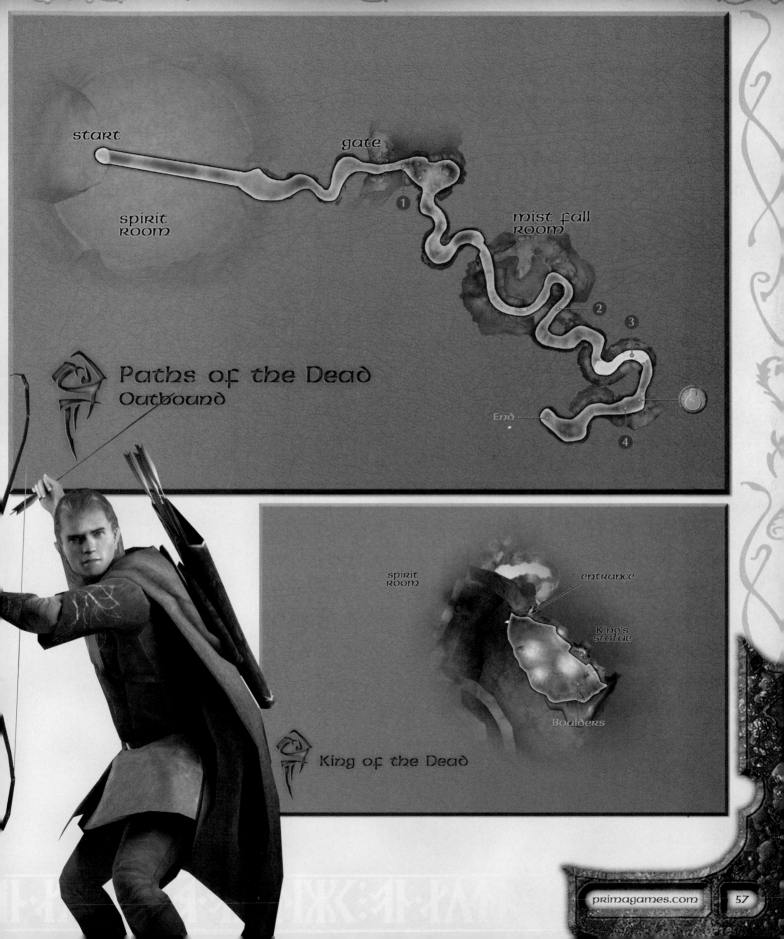

start

gate

spirit
ROOM

mist fall
ROOM

1

2

3

Paths of the Dead
Outbound

End

4

King of the Dead

spirit
ROOM

entrance

King's
statue

Boulders

King of the Dead

Facing the King of the Dead is your first boss challenge. There are a few stages to the battle where he uses different attacks. At first it's sword swings—the King will slash three times in quick succession. Use your Parry to knock the swipes away. After the third one, go on the offensive with three Speed Attacks, then go back to Parrying.

Trade blows with the King for the first round.

After a bit of swordplay your enemies will spiral into the ground and emerge near the entrance. Do **not** rush after him. He'll summon dead soldiers to his aid. If you stay far enough away they'll simply stand and wait for you. Use your Ranged Attack to draw one close to you and dispatch it with your melee weapon. Repeat this on all four dead soldiers.

DEVELOPER HINT

You can get a free shot at the King of the Dead if you use the killing move on him while he is burrowing into the ground.
—Ben Walker

The King of the Dead has many soldiers at his command.

When the last of his minions falls, the King spirals into the ground, emerging near you. He'll repeat the sword-strike pattern (three swings, then a pause), so take advantage and damage him. After a time he'll disappear, then reappear with new minions. This time he'll summon several archers.

Move in and use your Ranged Attack to dispatch them. When the final one falls, get ready for more swordplay with the King.

The archers will fall to your arrows.

CAUTION

Do not get close to the King of the Dead as he rises from the ground. He'll knock you over as he emerges.

After you damage the King a few more times, he changes up his attack. After a howl of rage, he sinks and then re-emerges in front of his statue. You end up behind a boulder. Stay there, and position yourself in the center. The King will send a wind that shatters first one side, then the other side of the boulder. The third blast will break the center, but you'll be safe, so stay put.

DEVELOPER HINT

Between wind attacks, jump out from behind the boulder and fire a fully-charged arrow.
—Ben Walker

The King is not pleased. Stay behind the center of the boulder or you'll be killed instantly.

After three blasts (which destroy the boulder), the King attacks again with his sword. This time the pattern is five sword strikes with a pause between the fourth and fifth strike. Parry the strikes and answer in kind. He'll sink a few passes later, then reappear to summon more soldiers.

As before, stay well back. The King brings up dead soldiers, with and without shields. Use your Ranged Attack to draw them to you one at a time. When the last one falls, the King comes close for more fencing. He's still using the five-stroke pattern, so be ready with the Parry button.

The King of the Dead can summon any dead soldiers he wishes. You'll see all three types as you battle the dead monarch.

After that it's another round with the King's minions. He has archers and shielded dead soldiers. Use the same methods that have served you before. When they're dispatched, the King comes up to you again. After the swordplay, he spins down but comes up next to his statue.

This is the cue that he is about to unleash his wind attack. Duck behind a boulder and stay there while he uses the wind to break it up.

Seek cover when the King calls forth the wind.

You have seen all the King's attacks and gambits. He'll repeat them, calling forth minions, attacking with his sword, and using wind to shatter boulders. Defend yourself and strike at the King during the sword-fighting. When you've done enough damage, the King of the Dead relents.

You've forced the King to yield, but now you must escape his realm.

ESCAPING THE PATHS OF THE DEAD

Now that the King of the Dead has been defeated, you and your companions must escape. The caverns are collapsing around you. If you dawdle on the path, the falling rocks will crush you. Sprint across the bridge and out of the spirit room.

DEVELOPER HINT

Fallen boulder chunks will slow you down. Try to run around them, not through them.
—Paul Mathus and Steve Szakal

Your only concern now is the falling rock. When the boulders hit the path, they'll break into smaller pieces that will delay you. Try to angle away from the falling rock as it crashes. Dodge the larger pieces on the path.

The larger chunks of rock in your way can slow you down, with fatal results.

As you may have guessed, you're backtracking over the path you took to find the King of the Dead. You quickly come to the gate near the fallen statue. Run through it and over the statue. You get a reprieve here from the falling ceiling; it won't stop, but it's not actively dropping stone on you. The way ahead is blocked by a specter-spawning bone wall. Battle dead soldiers to get by. Do this before the ceiling collapses. Take too long and you'll be buried.

Just past the gate, you encounter a fight. When the dead soldiers appear, the ceiling collapse slows.

DEVELOPER HINT

During battle, avoid using your Ranged Attack. Kill the enemies as fast as possible!
—Paul Mathus and Steve Szakal

The foes will swarm—keep your back to a wall to avoid them surrounding you. Use your combos to deal as much damage as possible during each attack. When the last dead soldier decomposes, the bone wall shatters. Immediately run through and keep moving.

Once again you'll need to dodge falling rock and the debris it leaves behind. Dust can obscure your view but don't stop pressing forward or you'll be buried.

You'll soon come to the stone bridge, where a bone wall again rises to block the way and dead soldiers spawn and surround you.

The collapsing tunnels are most hazardous when the view becomes cloudy.

The second battle point will pit you against fiercer foes.

These dead soldiers are tougher types. You'll face shielded ones as well as the dual-sword-wielding specters. Use your upgrades and special moves to keep yourself safe. There's time pressure: The battle must end before the collapse is final.

Once the bone wall breaks and no longer blocks your way, run! You'll quickly arrive in a mist-filled area. It slows your pace down to a walk. Keep watching for dropping rock, but pay close attention to the chunks on the floor. Getting stuck behind a piece of stone in the fog will bring you to a crawl.

DEVELOPER HINT

To get through the mist faster, turn around and press the Jump Back button repeatedly.
—Paul Mathus and Steve Szakal

The fog is doubly dangerous with obstacles that slow you down even more.

Past the fog, you meet up with your companions again. You'll be sealed into a small area with a bone wall that will generate many dead soldiers. You must fight them all off before the way will open. Luckily, your friends are a great help. They can keep some dead soldiers off balance and engaged as you fight. Several waves of enemies will emerge, so keep from being surrounded and use your best moves to carve a path.

DEVELOPER HINT

During the third bone wall battle, stay close to your companions for support.
—Paul Mathus and Steve Szakal

It can get thick during this battle.

The final wave of enemies is a trio of dual-sword-wielding dead soldiers. Once they fall, the bone wall will shatter, clearing the way out. Run forward into the safety of the open air.

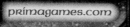

Southern Gate

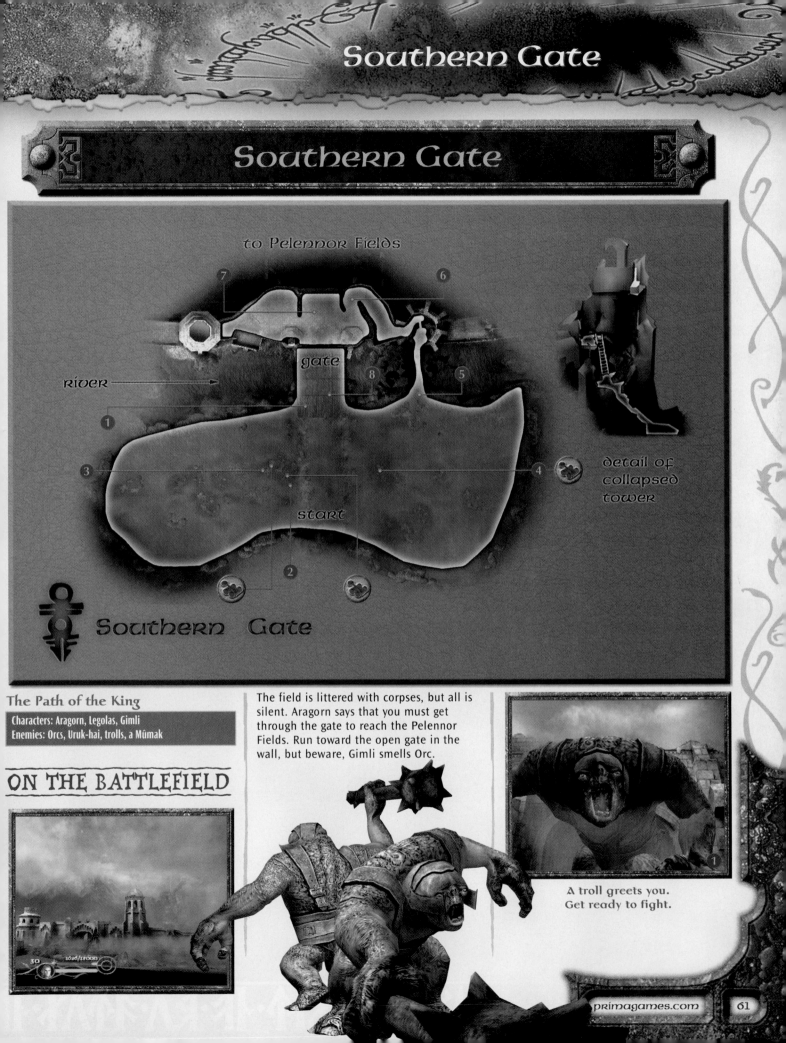

to Pelennor Fields

7

6

gate

river

8

5

1

3

4

detail of
collapsed
tower

start

2

Southern Gate

The Path of the King

Characters: Aragorn, Legolas, Gimli
Enemies: Orcs, Uruk-hai, trolls, a Mûmak

ON THE BATTLEFIELD

The field is littered with corpses, but all is silent. Aragorn says that you must get through the gate to reach the Pelennor Fields. Run toward the open gate in the wall, but beware, Gimli smells Orc.

A troll greets you.
Get ready to fight.

As soon as the doors slam shut and the troll leaps down from the wall, pull back and to your left. There is a spear stuck in the ground. Use the Action button to pick it up, then aim and throw it at the troll. It will slay him.

Orcs swarm onto the field and the fight begins. Your goal is to fire all the catapults on the field. To get to them, carve a path through an unending stream of foes.

Using the Orc Hewer move while playing Gimli is effective. It will sweep away a large group of Orcs, giving you a moment's peace.

The first two Orcs are west of the drawbridge. Use your power moves to strengthen your attacks and cut a swath to the siege weapons. Fire the first one and it shatters half of the tower to the east of the gate.

The first catapult will do half the job. You'll need to fire the second one to finish it.

Parrying is of the utmost importance, but you can't just block. Orcs keep coming and you need to get them out of the way, so don't forget to attack as well. Let your companions catch up to you and run interference. Move to the next catapult, hacking through the enemy as you go.

The second catapult shot will collapse the tower, giving you a way onto the wall.

Unless you are confident in your combat skills, quickly get those catapults fired. The battlefield is deadly with the crush of Orcs that collect on it and, for now, you don't want to spend much time there.

Run across the road you started on, to the third catapult. Fire it to weaken the troll on the wall. You'll encounter him later and it will help to have him injured when you meet again.

Battering the troll on the wall now pays off later.

It's time to move onto the wall. Run to the pile of rubble in front of the collapsed tower. It has formed a path up to the wall. Climb up the stones and you'll find a ladder up to the wall level.

Since no Orcs can emerge from the pile of rubble, you can put your back to it and wait for Orcs to attack you from the field. In this way, you can't get surrounded but can rack up experience in safety. There's some rough fighting ahead, so don't jeopardize your health.

The rubble pile is the next step.

After you're up there, more Orcs attack. Let them come to you on the narrow walkway so they can only attack one at a time. After you deal with them, push on and you'll see the troll. Use your Ranged Attack to dispatch him. Stay alert: A group of Orc soldiers will rush you from the other side of the wall as you deal with the troll.

DEVELOPER HINT

Powered-up Range Attacks will help you take down a troll much quicker.
—Steve Papoutsis

Fighting your enemies in a narrow space will help you stay alive.

Attack the big creature from afar.

Fight onto the main parapet, overlooking the gate. The scene will change. Prepare for the arrival of a huge beast of war, a Mûmak. On the wall, use Ranged Attacks to blast the battle platform on the Mûmak's back. However, the Orcs on the wall won't leave you alone as you fire and there are archers shooting at you from the Mûmak.

Balance Parrying with attacking. Attack the Orcs near you while attacking the battle platform. Your friends will help keep the Orcs mostly at bay, but they will require your personal attention as well.

DEVELOPER HINT

When the Mûmak appears, stay on your toes and use Parry often. Once you have an opening, fire arrows at the beast to destroy its armor.

—Steve Papoutsis

Destroy the three shield clusters on the battle platform. Then fire at the explosives.

To bring down the Mûmak, destroy the protective shields on its back, then fire shots to set off the explosives.

After the battle beast falls, waves of Orcs will come at you on the wall. The winch you must work to open the gate appears, but don't bother with it yet. First wipe the Orcs off the wall. After it's safe, go to the winch and use the Action button to work it. Turn it a few times to fully open the gate below.

Working the winch opens the gate you need to go through.

Before you leave the wall, move to the boiling cauldrons over the gate. Use the Action button to kick them over onto the Orcs. Send hot oil down on them to thin out the crowd. Head back to the rubble of the collapsed tower and climb down to the battlefield.

The boiling oil will destroy a few Orcs and make it easier for you to get through the gate.

Jump down the rubble and follow the river to the drawbridge where you were at the beginning of this level. The Orc horde has thinned, so you should be able to make it with minimum fuss. Deal with the Orcs left on the drawbridge.

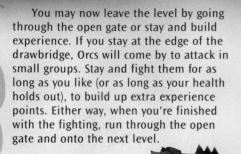

You may now leave the level by going through the open gate or stay and build experience. If you stay at the edge of the drawbridge, Orcs will come by to attack in small groups. Stay and fight them for as long as you like (or as long as your health holds out), to build up extra experience points. Either way, when you're finished with the fighting, run through the open gate and onto the next level.

It can be risky, but Orc-hunting at the bridge can boost your experience points.

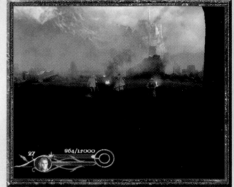

There are no **Checkpoints** in this level. So if you hang out on the bridge fighting and happen to get defeated, you'll have to play the whole thing again.

Minas Tirith—Top of the Wall

The Path of the Wizard

Character: Gandalf
Enemies: Uruk-hai, Fell Beast

ON THE WALL

Gandalf has come to Minas Tirith to strike at Sauron's forces. When the army attacks, the wizard is on the walls, defending them against the Orc hordes. It's not a battle he will win, but Gandalf can make his presence felt among his enemies.

The task at hand on the walls of Minas Tirith is to keep the Orcs at bay. They will try to use ladders and siege engines to get up on the parapet. Some will make it, but you need to keep the numbers down. In the upper-right corner, note the map of the

wall and the overrun meter. The map uses red dots to show you the location of ladders. The meter is a gauge of how many Orcs are on the wall. If it fills with red, the wall is overrun and you lose. Reduce the meter by knocking down ladders and destroying Orcs on the wall.

When a siege ladder goes up, a bright red dot appears on the map. After you push it away, the dot will clear off.

The meter and the map are invaluable tools for this level.

Your first task is twofold. Kick ladders away from the walls and battle the Orcs that make it to the walkway. Right away, ladders go up near you. A few Orcs need to be dispatched before you can get close enough to the ladders to push them away.

 You can kick away the ladders when you are near enough; you don't need to slay all the Orcs first. Pushing the ladders is the priority. Sweep any foes out of your way, then give the ladders a shove. If they are up for too long, more Orcs will scramble over the parapet and onto the walkway.

Immediately after the level starts, two ladders will be put up to your right. Run to the closest and use your Kick button to push it away. Carve through the Orcs and turn the corner to get at the second one. Knock it back and clean away any remaining Orcs.

DEVELOPER HINT

Ladders affect the overrun meter more, so go for them before going for surrounding Orcs.
—Michael Kirkbride

The map in this guide shows where ladders will appear. They can come back after you push one away. Keep an eye on the map and meter on your screen.

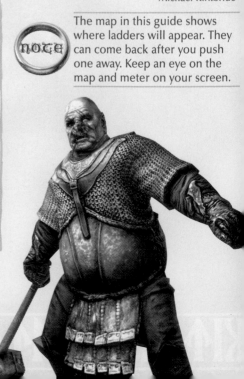

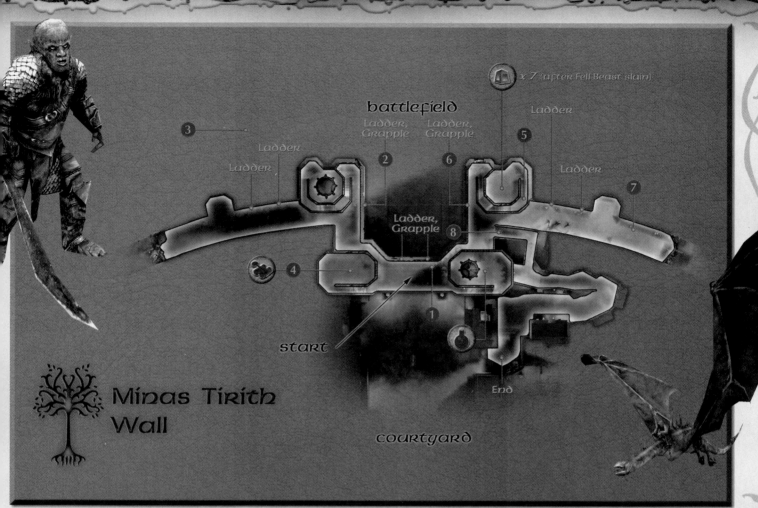

x 7 (after Fell Beast slain)

battlefield

Ladder, Grapple

Ladder, Grapple

Ladder

Ladder

Ladder

Ladder

Ladder, Grapple

3

2

6

5

7

8

4

1

start

End

Minas Tirith Wall

courtyard

The longer the ladders are in place, the more Orcs you'll have to deal with on the wall.

In the middle section of the wall, there are large grappling hooks. Step close to one and press the Action button to have Gandalf slide to a ledge beneath the wall. From there, you can run around the middle section and push away ladders without having to deal with Orcs. The grapples also become essential later on.

Don't spend too much time on the ledge. There are other matters to deal with.

If there is a moment of calm, when no ladders are marked on the map, patrol to make sure no foes are around. Moments of calm, however, will be rare if not nonexistent.

DEVELOPER HINT

Keep moving! Don't get bogged down in combat in any one area for too long. —Michael Becker

The walls are grueling. The fighting is almost constant.

Policing the wall is not your only task. After a time, you'll see a siege tower being pushed to the wall by a troll. If the tower reaches the wall, a stream of Orcs will pour out. The easiest way to deal with it is with a catapult. There's one on a tower to the east of the start point.

The towers are denoted on the map by a large blinking red dot. The first one will be obvious because you see a quick cutscene showing it being trundled to the wall. You'll have to spot the others for yourself, so keep an eye on the map on your screen.

The lumbering troll will push a siege tower to the wall, threatening your defense.

Climb the stairs to the catapult area and stand in the action circle near the winch. You'll be able to watch the tower as it moves closer. Press your Action button to fire the large weapon. After the shot, the Gondor soldiers will reload. You must wait for them to finish before pressing the Action button to fire the second shot. Two blows from the catapult will send the tower crashing to the ground.

Gandalf can direct the firing of the catapult. Waste no time destroying the structure.

Run to the wall and continue kicking ladders from the walls and destroying Orcs. Make a sweep of the area and frequently check the map in your screen's corner. Soon a second tower appears as a big blinking red dot on the map. It is near the wall's eastern arm.

You don't have a convenient catapult for this tower; you'll have to topple it with your Ranged Attack. You can fight over to the area it is headed for and fire at it from there, or climb halfway up the nearest tower's stairs and attack it from that vantage.

Once again, if the tower makes it to the wall, a horde of foes will jump out.

If you're quick enough, you can fire on the second tower from here.

To take it head-on, fire at the tower from in front of it.

After the second tower falls, a third one will appear on your map where the first one was destroyed. You can use the catapult again for this threat, so make your way to the weapon's tower and direct the team from there.

This time there's a wrinkle. After the catapult is launched once, a Nazgûl will appear on its flying mount. Target it with your Ranged Attack and fire quickly. If you don't drive it off, the Ringwraith will carry away one of the soldiers manning the catapult.

The Ringwraith will come after the catapult soldiers if you don't do something.

As it collapses, the Nazgûl 's mount wrecks part of the wall.

When the Ringwraith falls, it crashes into the wall, crushing stones and blocking your path to the eastern arm. Fire the catapult a second time to destroy the tower, then rush down to the wall.

Despite your efforts, a tower will reach the eastern arm of the wall, disgorging a horde of enemies. Because the way is now blocked by rubble, you'll need to use the grapples to reach the ledge. Climb down, run to the rope closest to the tower, and climb back up.

Use the grapples and the ledge to circumvent the blocked portion of the wall.

DEVELOPER HINT

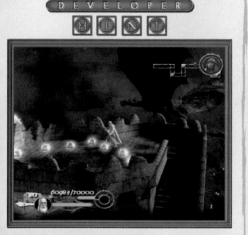

Killing the Fell Beast will reveal seven Elfstones on top of the front right tower.   —Bret Robbins

After grabbing the bonus Elfstones, race to where the tower is moored and a large number of foes meets you. Use your upgrades and moves (such as the Orc Hewer) to clear them away. After the initial group is gone, more will climb up through the tower unless you smash it with Ranged Attacks. When you have a moment to spare, use the Ranged Attack to hit the tower. A few strikes and it will fall.

If your meter is in good shape and you're confident in your fighting ability, hold off on destroying the tower. Let the Orcs come up it so you can defeat them and gain experience points as you go. Other foes are still climbing up ladders, so watch the meter. When it gets near full, destroy the tower to move on to the next part of the level.

The tower can dispense a large number of enemies.

TO THE COURTYARD

When the siege tower falls, you'll see a group of trolls forcing the doors of the wall with a battering ram. This signals the end of the wall's defense. Now follow the human soldiers as they flee downstairs. Mop up any Orc groups on the wall (if your health is good) then find the top of the stairs.

The stairs begin near the rubble caused by the falling Fell Beast. Follow the crowd of soldiers to avoid dangers as you run.

This is the top of the stairs, now open for you to make your escape.

The crush of soldiers is confusing, but keep moving along the path. A small archway shows up ahead after you go around a hairpin turn. Don't head for it, as it will collapse in a second. Follow the crowd into the courtyard. You'll see a cutscene of the gates shattering. Gandalf alone stands unharmed and the level ends.

Shelob's Lair

Shelob's Lair

the maze

orc camp

inner lair

Checkpoint

start

overpass

Checkpoint

The Path of the Hobbits

Character: Sam
Enemies: spiders, Orcs, shielded Orcs, archer Orcs, Shelob (Boss)

THROUGH THE MAZE

Tricked by Gollum, Sam and Frodo are caught in the lair of a monstrous and ageless giant spider, Shelob. The hobbits become separated and Sam must find his master.

The first obstacle is the maze. This network of tunnels is difficult to navigate, but use the map to guide your steps. You'll want to collect several significant objects on your way through. Two Elfstones wait in dead ends. Seek them out for the experience points.

The closest Elfstone is easily found. Follow the wall to Sam's right after the level starts.

The smaller spiders are as hazardous as the larger ones.

The torches mark the way out of the maze.

The maze isn't benign. Large spiders attack you as you go. These creatures are most dangerous in packs. The most effective attack is the Final Judgment move. If used properly, Sam can defeat a spider with only three button presses. When faced with a group of monsters, Parry until all of them have had an attack, then unleash the Final Judgment on the closest. Repeat the process, parrying, then attacking. It may take some time, but you can keep yourself safe with this technique.

The way to the green health vial is treacherous.

There's a green health vial in one of the dead ends. Grab it before you head for the maze's exit, as you'll want to be healthy for the next section of the lair. You'll have to negotiate a path around the smaller spiders, so take it easy as you walk.

After you're ready, find the passage at the back of the maze that leads to the Orc camp. You can use the map to guide you, but it is recognizable by the two torches in brackets on either side of the passage. Spiders will be around, so deal with them, then examine the way forward.

Use the torches as weapons against the larger spiders. Use your Action button to grab one and throw it at your attacker.

TO THE INNER LAIR

A scrambling mass of smaller spiders blocks the path. Grab a torch and toss it in the midst of the scurrying creatures and they'll part, clearing the way for you to get by.

Beyond that, near another torch bracket, a trio of spiders drops from the ceiling. Destroy the monsters, then grab the torch. Throw it at the web, blocking the passage ahead. The web will burn away (wait for it to finish before moving forward). Continue on.

A large group of spiders is trouble. Be patient and you can fight your way through.

When you pick up an Elfstone, spiders will drop to attack. Keep your back to a wall and use the system described before to defeat them.

At points in the lair you'll come across a veritable carpet of small spiders. Don't try to walk through them: They bite! The damage may not seem like much, but if you stay in contact with them it quickly adds up.

You can use the torch to fight spiders here, but it can leave you open to attack.

The path leads to the Orc camp, a large group of Orcs complaining around a fire. You can use your Elven Cloak to sneak in. Move right to find a torch bracket. Before you use it, however, spiders attack. Deal with them, then grab the torch. Aim it at the Orc standing under one of the bodies hanging from the ceiling. When you toss it, the torch will hit the body (with a bit of luck), sending it down amongst your foes to start a conflagration.

Try that with the other body, as well. If you can't hit them, no worries; throw torches to deal with the foes below and slay the ones that make it up to you with your sword.

After the spiders are gone, you can turn your attention to the Orcs.

 You can also use the Elven Cloak to sneak by the camp. This can be risky, however, because you'll have to do it in two stages and if you're caught in the open you have a good chance of being surrounded.

Beyond the Orc camp, a couple of Orcs are near a torch bracket. Past them, a pair of spiders are locked in a struggle with a pair of Orcs. You can use the torch nearby to destroy the combatants or use your Ranged Attack or Melee Attack to deal with the rest.

Thin out the enemies before you attack.

Now you'll have a choice of paths, left or right. To Sam's left is a dead end that overlooks a stone bridge. A few archers on it will fire at you. You can fight them with Ranged Attacks and/or torches. However, the speed at which they fire ensures you'll take some damage. Leave it for later.

To the right you'll come to an open area with the main path leading right into a large group of Orcs. A smaller path leads up. Use your Elven Cloak and move up the smaller path. Grab the torch in the bracket and hurl it toward the body hanging from the ceiling.

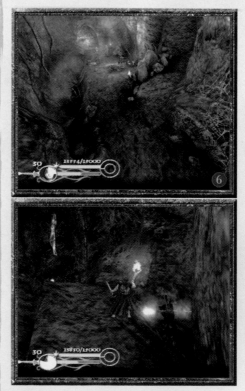

Sneak up the path to the right, then use the torch to bring the body down from the ceiling.

The resulting fire will injure or destroy the Orcs at the top of the path. Move to the top and dispatch any survivors. When it's clear, use your Action button on the stack of rocks. Sam will push the rocks onto the group of Orcs below, clearing your way with minimum fuss.

Go down and cross the open area toward the tunnel leading out. Before you are through, several spiders attack. Back up and use the torches and fire pots to destroy them or use Final Judgment.

Tumble the stones to clear the way, then move deeper into the lair.

Past the tunnel, you'll come to the bridge you saw the archers on earlier. A cutscene reveals the giant spider Shelob as she scuttles under the bridge. Sam is worried. Luckily, you've just hit a **Checkpoint**.

CHECKPOINT

After the *Checkpoint*, you'll find a few more Orcs to dispatch.

As you cross the bridge, you'll run into more Orcs. Use the nearby torch to drop another flaming body on them or use your sword skills. After they're gone, move on to an area almost overrun with spiders.

A couple of big ones will attack near a brace of torches. Take care of them, then examine the way ahead. A large swath of small spiders is blocking the way. Grab a torch and fling it at them. That will move half of them out of the way. Grab the second torch and throw that further along. With both brands burning, you'll have a path through the little critters. Duck through quickly, before the torches burn out.

It takes two torches to get through this swarm.

Past that carpet of spiders is another clear area. A pair of large spiders drops in for a battle. Hack at them, then consider the way ahead. There's a torch to your left and another surrounded by a layer of small spiders. You need to get to the second torch, so pick up the first one and toss it at the spiders. When they part, run to the second torch.

After you reach the torch, grab it and toss it at the web blocking the tunnel ahead. Run through the path you opened through the spiders. You can walk around the spider swarm and go through the tunnel you opened.

After a fight against large spiders, use torches to deal with the smaller spiders and burn your way through a web.

More large spiders attack you at the cave mouth, so be on guard. In the tunnel, you'll fight a pair of Orcs. Use the handy torches to take them down.

In the next area, you'll have smaller spiders with which to deal. Two paths face you, one straight ahead and one leading up (similar to the open area with the rockfall you caused earlier). Grab the nearest torch and aim it at the cluster of small spiders to the right. Throw to clear them away and head up the path.

Two choices: straight ahead or up. Go up first.

You'll be ambushed by several large spiders. Use your Final Judgment and general combat skills to emerge victorious, then continue up the raised path. You'll find a torch bracket at the top, overlooking the other path. Grab the torch and aim it at the mouth of the tunnel leading out. It's covered with webbing that you need to burn away. Toss the torch, then head down.

From here you can get rid of the webbing blocking your forward progress.

Use the torch at the bottom to get through the small spiders and to the start of this area. Take the torch you used to get on the upper path and aim it at the cluster of spiders to the left. When the creatures scatter, move ahead on the lower path.

Walk this path in stages, because bands of small spiders cover sections of the walkway. When you reach the first clear spot, Orc archers come out of the newly opened tunnel to harass you. Parry away their shots and use your Ranged Attack to deal with them.

The archers can be troublesome. Use your Ranged Attacks or thrown torches to get rid of them.

Deal with the archers at long range. If you attempt to rush at them, you'll get caught or pushed into the middle of the swarm of small spiders.

After the Orcs are gone, you can continue negotiating your way across the path. Grab the nearby torch and spin it into the midst of the spiders blocking your way to clear them out. Move to the next clear area and repeat the torch process to pass the final band of small spiders.

Larger spiders will attack at the mouth of the tunnel you burned open. Keep from getting surrounded, but don't back up into the smaller spiders. After it's clear, move forward to the opening at the end of the tunnel. Get ready. You're in for a long fight.

SHELOB

Shelob has gotten hold of Frodo. She's wrapping him tight.

The enormous spider is not a kind creature. You'll have to work fast to save the Ring-bearer.

10 Shelob

Shelob is a difficult enemy to get a handle on. Her many legs are always flailing to move her about or attack you. It can be unclear which is which in the heat of the battle, making it difficult to decide when to attack.

Run up to the creature and begin your assault. Her back is to you, so you get a free hit. Try the Orc Hewer move. It can deal a lot of damage, especially if you get two of them off.

Your first strike can take Shelob unaware.

After that you don't get any free shots. Press your advantage as long as you can. Eventually the monster finds her footing and comes back at you. Parry her leg strikes (three in a row), then come back with your own hits. After you damage her a few times, you'll get a cutscene showing Sam putting out one of the vile creature's eyes.

D E V E L O P E R
H I N T

When you see Shelob scuttling toward you, charge in to meet her with Speed and Fierce Attacks, then quickly jump back. Repeat this pattern to finish her off quickly.
—Steve Papoutsis

When you've done enough damage, you'll succeed in stabbing one of Shelob's eyes. It's not a death blow, but it will get her attention.

Shelob's Lair

After Sam strikes that mighty blow, Shelob retreats to the wall and calls forth some large spiders to attack you. You've dealt with this type of monster before. There are several of them and they attempt to surround you.

Time is of the essence. You need to slay them before Shelob jumps down, because it will be easier to fight Shelob without her minions crawling around. Rush the first spider you see and use the Final Judgment move. Repeat that with the next spider, and so on. If you're quick enough, you can dispatch a number of them before the others are close enough to harm you. Be bold. Parry an attack and counter with the Final Judgment. This keeps you healthy.

DEVELOPER HINT

Once Shelob retreats onto a wall, do not engage her; instead finish off the large spiders first by using Fierce Attacks to flip them over, and the Finishing move to kill them. If you make a mistake and use Ranged Attacks on Shelob when she is on the wall, you will have a much harder time finishing this fight.
—Steve Papoutsis

Charge into your foes to keep them from swarming you.

When the spiders are destroyed (or enough time passes), Shelob leaps from her perch and tries to slam you to the ground. You have to be moving soon after she leaves the wall to avoid it, so be ready for it.

If she misses you, the impact leaves her flat for a moment. Dart in and take your swings while she's stunned.

Having Shelob knocked flat is a rare opportunity. Take advantage of it.

When she recovers, Shelob will scuttle toward you, take several strikes, then scuttle back. Parry her attacks then strike as she's moving in or moving away.

Orc Hewer is a good move here. However, you may get interrupted by Shelob's attacks. The timing is tricky. Rush at the creature's head, getting in close. This keeps you out of range of her legs (until she moves again) and allows you to get off an attack or two.

Getting next to Shelob's head is a good vantage point for your attacks.

When the giant spider has taken enough, she'll retreat to the wall and send more of her brood to fight you. Use the same tactics, charging and attacking with Final Judgment, to thin their ranks.

When Shelob leaps down again, the sparring that follows is grueling. At times she'll sidestep to avoid you, circling as you try to catch up. To get her, cut across her path and swipe as she moves.

When you've made enough hits on the monster, a cutscene shows Sam hacking off part of one of her forelegs. This drives the spider into a frenzy, and she bolts, knocking you over in the process, and gallops around the Inner Lair.

DEVELOPER HINT

When Shelob begins her rampage, stay clear of her. Use the Jump Back button to avoid her attacks.
—Steve Papoutsis

Sam wields his sword well and Shelob pays the price, but when she charges, there's no avoiding getting bowled over.

After Sam regains his feet, you can dodge Shelob as she dashes around the area. After a few moments, she'll retreat to the wall and call out a large group of spiders to come after you.

You can use the same tactics; don't end up surrounded by the beasts. Keep to the edges and take on the one closest to you.

After you clear them away, Shelob will join the fray. Her attacks are less effective, because she's missing one of her forelegs, but you still need to be alert as you trade blows.

Shelob makes a dive at Sam, but he's ready, plunging his sword into the creature's abdomen.

Half her attacking legs are gone, but Shelob is still dangerous.

Be ready for another wave of Shelob's brood while she sulks on the wall. This one is a large group ,so don't rush into their midst. Pick away at the ones on the edges, working your way through them.

Shelob is weak by now. Continue crowding her, getting close enough to use your Orc Hewer or strike at her with Speed Attacks. When you drain away the last of her health bar, a cutscene shows Sam's victory.

Wounded, though not killed, the beast staggers off to hide and tend to herself.

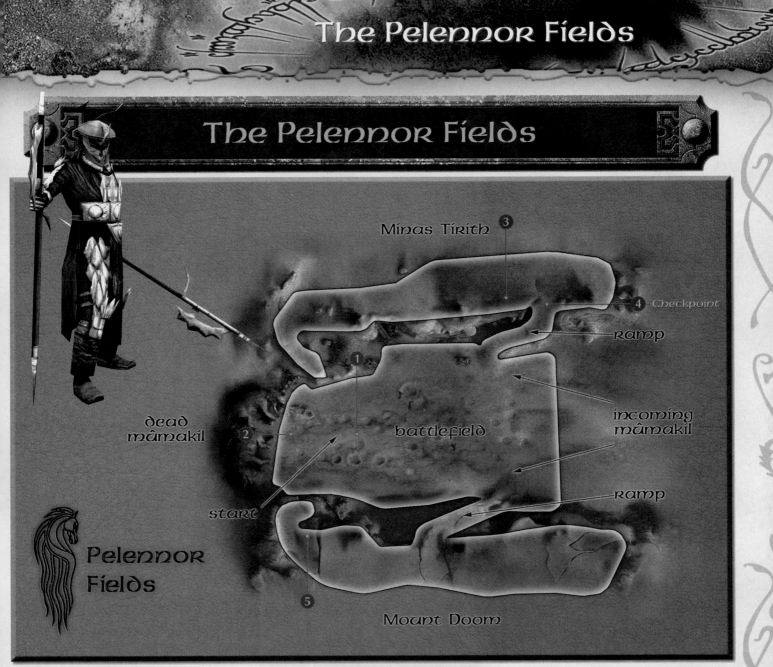

The Pelennor Fields

Minas Tirith ③

④ Checkpoint

ramp

①

incoming mûmakil

dead mûmakil ②

battlefield

ramp

start

⑤

Pelennor Fields

Mount Doom

The Path of the King

Characters: Aragorn, Legolas, Gimli
Enemies: Easterlings, Shielded Easterlings, Easterling Champions, Uruk-hai, *mûmakil*, Witch-king

ON THE FIELD

Having walked the Paths of the Dead and passed through the southern gate, Aragorn, Legolas, and Gimli find themselves in the midst of a pitched battle on the Pelennor Fields. The Rohirrim are engaged with the army out of Mordor and the Easterling troops. The outlook is grim.

The three companions are in the thick of things.

You are thrown into fierce combat from the beginning. You have allies in the riders of Rohan, but there are two sets of enemies: Orcs and Easterlings. We recommend using Legolas for your first trip through the fields. His speed can keep the foes at bay and get you out of a swarm. Gimli is able to carve through crowds with a degree of ease. His slow speed is balanced by sweeping cuts.

Initially avoid the Champions and stick to the weaker enemies until you get into Perfect Mode.
—Chris Ferriera

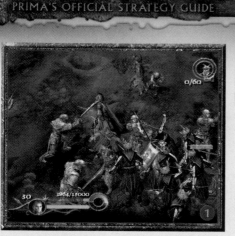

The crush of people on the field can be overwhelming.

Notice the counter in the upper-right corner. You must slay 60 enemies before moving to the next part of the level. It may seem an easy task, given the number of foes. However, the Easterlings have a large number of shielded soldiers and soldiers wielding two halberds. Both types of enemy require a Fierce Attack to break through their defenses before you can damage them.

 NOTE You don't have to personally defeat all 60 of the enemies. Your allies will take care of some of them.

The shielded and dual-weapon-wielding enemies are tough to destroy under such hectic conditions.

While it is tempting to simply wade into battle, weapons swinging, that's not the smartest tactic. Keep to the edges as you fight, letting the foes come to you. This reduces the number of enemies you have to deal with at one time. If you end up surrounded, Parry continuously until allies arrive. If no help comes, use Speed Attacks and attempt to break out and run to a clearer area.

Your companions will come to your aid if they are able.

Continue circling the edges, taking down soldiers that come at you, moving in closer to the main fray when the area is clear. You shouldn't be short of company. The Easterlings and Orcs will come to you as you fight.

THE MÛMAKIL

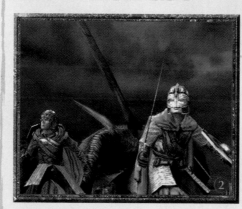

Éowyn and Merry make an appearance on the battlefield.

When the counter is full, Éowyn and Merry reveal themselves on the field. They are posted at one end, near the dead *mûmakil*. More war beasts are coming, however, and headed straight for your stout allies.

You'll be brought automatically to a cliff overlooking the battlefield. It's a **Checkpoint**, so you won't have to battle the hordes again if anything goes wrong. Your new task is to bring down the *mûmakil* threatening Éowyn and Merry.

DEVELOPER HINT

After destroying the first Mûmak, you must cross the battlefield to fight the second. The way down is between the middle and far left ballista.

—Nina Dobner

The Mûmak will destroy anything in its path.

CHECKPOINT

If you run low on ammo for your Ranged Attack, find a quiver at the top of the ramp for either of the two cliffs you'll visit.

After you're up on the cliff, run to your left. You'll find a loaded ballista and a view of the Mûmak. You can use your Ranged Attack to destroy the beast's armor as it lumbers in, or wait for it to line up with the ballista, then fire that siege weapon. It will take a few ballista shots to fell a Mûmak, so use your Ranged Attack at first. You won't have other distractions while fighting this initial Mûmak, so you can experiment with the ballistae (there are three on the cliff), war pikes (stuck in the ground between the ballistae), and your Ranged Attack.

Beware of the archers firing arrows off the Mûmak's war platform. Parry them away before attacking.

The first Mûmak can fall easily to your Ranged Attack. Destroy its armor, then target the explosives on its platform.

Shortly after the beast falls, a second Mûmak appears. This one is too far from the cliff you're on—run to the second cliff to deal with it. Find the ramp (marked with a triangular flag on a staff) and head down into the battlefield.

Locate the staff with a flag and you'll find the ramp. Run down it.

You don't have time to mess around on the field, so cut straight away from the ramp when you hit bottom. Enemies may try to engage you, but dodge them and find the other ramp that leads to the opposite cliff. If you hit the other side without finding the ramp, simply run alongside the cliff face until you see it.

After you're up there, use the ballistae and Ranged Attacks to topple the Mûmak. This time, foes on the cliff give you trouble. Your companions will run interference for some of them, but you'll have to give others your full attention. Additionally, the archers on the Mûmak are firing at you, and you have to shoot the ballistae at the right time. It can be hectic.

Fire the ballista as soon as the Mûmak is lined up in front of it.

DEVELOPER

Stick to the parapets at the end of the cliff sides for shooting at the Witch-king, where the unlimited-range power-ups are found.   —Chris Ferriera

When the second Mûmak drops, you see a disturbing sight. The Witch-king swoops over Merry and Éowyn. Aragorn shouts that they must be saved. Rush to the end of the cliff nearest the pair of allies on the ground. Enemy fighters on the cliff may make this difficult, but dodge them to get to the other end.

After you reach the other end, clear some foes away and use your Ranged Attack to drive off the Nazgûl. There's a health bar in the upper-left corner for Merry and Éowyn. Make sure it doesn't empty. Another health bar hovers in the upper-right corner for the Witch-king. That's the one you need to drain.

Your priority is to keep Éowyn and Merry safe. The Witch-king adds a wrinkle to the task.

DEVELOPER HINT

Only the Witch-king and *mûmakil* can hurt Merry and Éowyn, so do not focus on the Uruk-hai and Easterlings around them.
—Chris Ferriera

You can drive the foe away after dealing it enough damage. When the Witch-king is out of range, however, another Mûmak shows up. Depending on which cliff it is nearest, you may need to run across the battlefield.

DEVELOPER HINT

Pay attention to the torches and banners in the cutscenes, as they let you know what side the next Mûmak is coming in from.
—Chris Ferriera

Deal with the Mûmak, then the Witch-king when he comes to harass Éowyn and Merry. The battle will go back and forth between the two large enemies. Your limitation will be Éowyn and Merry's health meter: If they die, you'll lose the level.

Be in position before the Witch-king descends on Merry and Éowyn. If you fire your Ranged Attack when he shows up, you prevent some of the damage he'll do to your friends. This is especially important with Gimli, because his Ranged Attack is slow to develop.

When you've done enough damage to the Nazgûl Lord, his flying mount crashes to the ground. Your active part in this level ends.

After the Witch-king falls from the Fell Beast, you can breathe easier.

The Witch-king faces Éowyn, unaware that she is a woman.

No man alive can defeat the Nazgûl Lord, but Éowyn is no man and she ends his existence.

Despite victory, the advance of more *mûmakil* makes Gimli nervous.

The army of the dead comes forth to save the living. The battle is won.

Minas Tirith—Courtyard

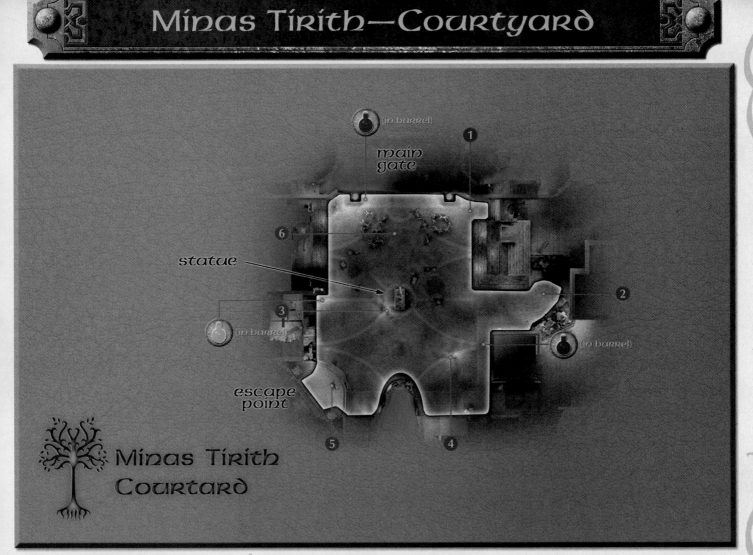

(in barrel)

main
gate

1

6

statue

3

(in barrel)

2

(in barrel)

escape
point

5

4

Minas Tirith
Courtard

The Path of the Wizard

Character: Gandalf
Enemies: Orcs, shielded Orcs, archer Orcs, Uruk-hai, trolls, Uruk-hai Champions

THE REAR GUARD ACTION

Having been routed from the walls, the people of Minas Tirith are fleeing into their city. Gandalf is there to fight a holding action and save as many citizens as he can.

You begin in the courtyard with a group of Orcs bearing down on you. You must fight until 200 citizens have made it through the escape point. There are soldiers to help with bows but you must do the majority of the fighting.

The first group has only one shielded foe. Deal with him first.

This level is one long battle from beginning to end. There will be little rest after it gets started, so get comfortable. The fleeing women of Gondor come from two points: one near the main gate, and the other is the path you followed at the end of the level on top of the Minas Tirith wall.

The people you are trying to save come from here...

...and here.

The escape point is a door in the lower-east corner of the courtyard. The enemy will attempt to attack the citizens and their defenders. Dispatch them so they don't slow the stream of refugees. Slay the foe so the citizens can get out fast.

The first few waves of Orcs come by type. The second group is made up of shielded Orcs. You don't have to wade into the middle of a group, you can hang back until they spread out so you don't get mobbed. This keeps you healthy as the fight progresses.

DEVELOPER HINT

Archers can't hurt shielded enemies, so break enemies' shields and let the Gondor archers finish them off.
—Chris Ferriera

Your Fierce Attack will get through shields and armor.

Use your parrying skills during this battle. The level is one long skirmish and there aren't a lot of healing vials around. You need to stay alive. So if you haven't developed your blocking abilities yet, this level will be a trial by fire.

The war pikes at two points of the map are effective against your enemy. Even though they regenerate, harbor them for the larger threats later in the level. You will be kept informed when those threats appear.

This is one basket of war pikes.

This is the other.

DEVELOPER HINT

Shoot the Orc archers instead of trying to fight them up close. This saves you from taking a lot of damage.
—Chris Ferriera

After a couple more waves, the Uruk-hai show up in force. They take more effort to destroy, but use your upgrade moves to deal with them.

Soon you notice a line of Orc archers near the main gate. They pepper the courtyard with flaming arrows. Use your Ranged Attack to pick them off. At this point, your shots should be powerful enough to slay them without being charged up. Fire quickly, but be sure your shots aren't blocked by the statue in the middle of the courtyard.

DEVELOPER HINT

Use Gandalf's special ability to make short work of large groups of enemies.
—Chris Ferriera

Take care of the archers posthaste.

Orcs in the doorway can
cause trouble for the refugees.

After you clear away the first wave of
archers, another one appears. Once again
they're stationed by the main gate in a line,
and once again you should use rapid shots of
your Ranged Attack to dispense with them.

Several more waves of foot soldier Orcs
sweep in. Use your moves to clear them
away. Periodically run to the escape point
to check that no Orcs are camping out in it,
wreaking havoc on the Gondorian women.

Watch where the Gondor archers
are firing arrows. If they are
shooting at the escape point, an
enemy is there being bothersome.

It's only a matter of time before an
Uruk-hai Champion shows up. This bruiser,
armed with two maces, is armored. Use
Fierce Attacks to knock away his protection
before you can defeat him. As with the
shielded Orcs, you can knock away his
armor, then let the Gondorian archers
whittle him down. Run from the Champion
and attack weaker enemies. He may chase
you but there's a good chance that your
allies will be able to damage him.

DEVELOPER HINT

One war pike will knock the armor off a Champion,
and a subsequent war pike hit will kill him.
—Chris Ferriera

A second Champion will appear after
the first. A shielded Orc is often alongside
and the two of them can tag-team you,
with disastrous results. Maneuver so you
can separately deal with them. Specifically,
get near one of the Gondor archers who
may run interference for you.

There will be more Uruk-hai
Champions later. Many more.

DEVELOPER HINT

Watch out for enemies who gather around the stairs
where the Gondorian women are leaving.
—Chris Ferriera

Check on the points where the women
originate from time to time. Often you'll
find a group of creatures harassing your
charges. Clear them out to help the citizens.

The Uruk-hai Champions keep coming.
Use the Fierce Attack to strip their defenses.
They can be most dangerous if they're in a
crowd of lesser Orcs. The smaller foes will
keep you off balance and unable to block
the Champions' crushing blows. Escape such
mobs and use your Ranged Attack to thin
them out before they can regroup.

A gang of Orcs can clog up
the stream of refugees.

When 150 Gondorian women have reached safety, things get worse for the defenders of Minas Tirith. A trio of enormous trolls storms through the main gate. A cutscene introduces the horrors. When you regain control of Gandalf, rush to the basket of war pikes and use them to fell two of the beasts. You may have to cut away a few Orcs before you get a clear shot.

If you miss with the pikes, either run to the next cache of pikes or use your Ranged Attack to bring them down. Make the trolls your priority. Deal with them quickly because more Uruk-hai Champions are on their way.

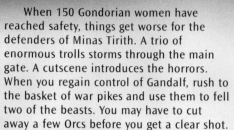

The trolls can't be left to wander around the courtyard. Use the war pikes or your Ranged Attack to stop them.

After you dispatch the first three trolls, deal with the Orcs closest to you. More than likely, a Champion will have sought you out first. Take him down, then move to the basket of war pikes farthest from the main gate. You will see a troll that's come down the stairs behind fleeing women. Use a war pike to fell him.

The situation in the courtyard can spiral out of control past this point. Don't feel that you have to destroy every foe in the space. Your job at this point is staying alive. Use the health items if you need them and avoid getting swarmed. You'll still need to fight, but don't charge into the middle of things or you'll be quickly overwhelmed.

The final fights are crazed melees.

Keep a handle on things with judicious use of your Ranged Attack and the war pikes. Use the pole arm weapons to deal with trolls and any Champions that come after you. The most important thing is to not let yourself get surrounded.

When the counter reaches 180, you're in good shape. Stay to the outskirts and harass the enemy from there. Keep alive and the women will continue to escape. After the counter hits 200, you will have fulfilled your duties and the level will end.

TIP

If the counter is at 190 or more and things are getting desperate, stay in one place and constantly Parry. It's not heroic, but as long as no trolls come by, you can last long enough to end the level.

The Orcs have overrun the courtyard.

Gandalf signals a retreat. Minas Tirith has inner walls that must now be defended.

The outer area now belongs to the forces of Mordor. But perhaps there will be aid coming for the White City....

Cirith Ungol

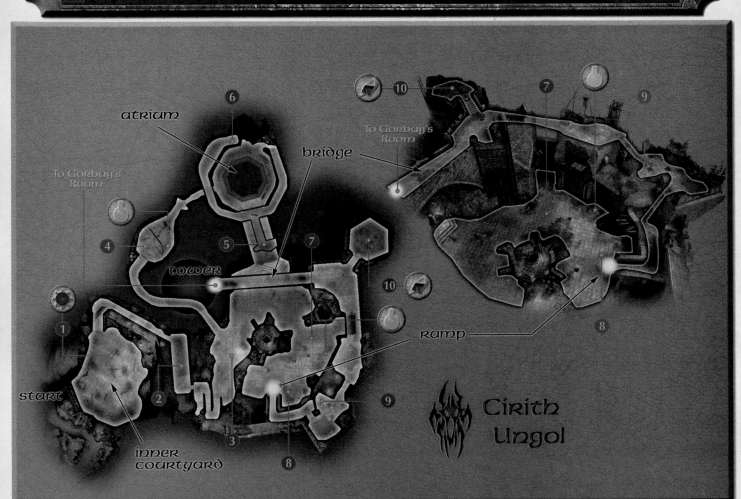

atrium

bridge

To Gorbag's Room

To Gorbag's Room

tower

ramp

start

inner courtyard

Cirith Ungol

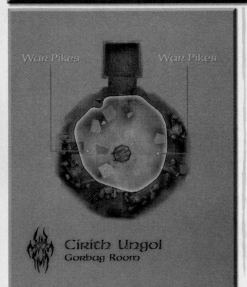

War Pikes   War Pikes

Cirith Ungol
Gorbag Room

The Path of the Hobbits

Character: Sam
Enemies: Uruk-hai, Orcs, shielded Orcs, Orc Champions, Gorbag (Boss)

ONE AGAINST MANY

With Frodo in the tower of Cirith Ungol, it's a given that Sam will make his way there. He sneaks to the gate and finds that the Orcs inside are in an uproar. They've turned against each other and the garrison has erupted into chaos. It's possible that Sam has a chance to find his master. Unfortunately, it will mean getting by a lot of Orcs.

DEVELOPER
H I N T

You will get more experience from killing enemies with traps than with just regular combat.
—Ben Walker

Your task is to wend your way into Cirith Ungol and defeat 80 Orcs as you go. You're first faced with the inner courtyard. There are several Orcs and a winch that lowers a ramp. You can use one to get rid of a lot of the other. Run a little way into the courtyard (without being seen) and use your special ability to pull the Elven Cloak around Sam and hide him from view. Get to the winch and press the Action button to lower the ramp, crushing several Orcs.

Taking out a group of Orcs with the ramp is a good idea. Afterward, you'll have to fight a larger foe.

The ramp trick won't completely clear out the room. You'll still have an Orc and an Orc Champion to deal with. A pair of battling Orcs will also come down the bridge, but won't pay attention to you as they fight. Take out the smaller enemy first, then face off with the Champion. Use your Fierce Attacks to knock away his armor, then use special moves to take him down.

DEVELOPER HINT

Pick your fights. Don't rush into large battles until you have thinned the Orc ranks. —Michael Becker

After that's done, you can go after the Orcs fighting each other. Wait until one is knocked down, then use your Killing move on him and use Final Judgment on the one still standing. When it's clear, head up the ramp you lowered and follow the walkway at the top. A pair of foes charge you, so Parry their blows and attack with Final Judgment to get them out of the way.

The Final Judgment move is effective for Sam when faced with the Orcs of Cirith Ungol. It allows him to dispatch foes with minimum fuss. Be careful, however, when working against tightly packed groups. Use other moves (like Speed Attacks) to keep them at bay.

A tunnel leads off the walkway. Follow it until another pair of Orcs and an Orc Champion appear at the opposite end. Let the Orcs come to you and deal with them one at a time. When they're gone, rush the Champion but use the Elven Cloak (which is recharged by now) before you get in range of his attacks. Sneak behind him and use the Finishing move to get an Instant Kill. This is safer than a head-to-head battle.

The sneaky approach is good for your health.

Outside the tunnel is a staircase leading down to a large open area. From the sounds you can tell there's a huge battle going on, though you can't see it yet. Grab the war pike in front of you and use it to spear the Orc at the top of the steps. Head down to the first landing to find the pair of creatures battling there. Dart past them or use Ranged Attacks to defeat them. Or wait until one is knocked down before joining the fight.

A convenient war pike helps defeat the closest Orc.

Beyond the bottom of the stairs is a battle royale between the Orcs of Cirith Ungol. Luckily they won't attack you en masse because they're busy fighting each other. If you get too close, they'll take swings at you. Because you have to slay 80 of them, defeat the ones closest to you, then find the iron brazier farther on. Use your Action button to tip it and the scattered coals will dispatch the nearest Orcs.

First deal with the closest foes, then spill the hot coals.

The way ahead is packed with enemies, so take a less treacherous route. Find the passage to the left of the brazier you used. It leads to a shielded Orc (use your Fierce Attack to get by him) and a room in a tower.

Another pitched battle is being fought in the room, but again, only one Orc will attack you. Dispatch him, then tip the brazier nearest you. When it's done its work, other Orcs remain. Fight them or rush to the brazier farther on and tip it. Clean up what's left and press on down the next passage.

Turn over both braziers to thin out the enemies in this room.

You'll reach the atrium where another huge battle is raging. Use the Elven Cloak and move to the left and up the stairs without being noticed. Climb the stairs using the war pikes you find along the way to dispatch the Orcs blocking your ascent. Halfway up, you'll see a landing with a passage leading off. Dispatch the Orcs on the landing and follow the passage.

It ends on a balcony overlooking part of the open area you were in earlier. A cauldron of boiling oil awaits you. Use the Action button to tip it onto the combatants below. Spill it several times to make sure you've cleared out every Orc you can, then head to the stairs.

Pour the oil a few times
on the area below.

Continue climbing the staircase until you find another landing. An Orc Champion is guarding it, but you can use war pikes to weaken him. If your special ability has recharged, use your Elven Cloak and back-stab him for an easy victory. After the Champion is out of the way, find the rope at the back of the landing. Stand near it and use the Action button to cut the tether, sending a huge chandelier crashing down on the Orcs.

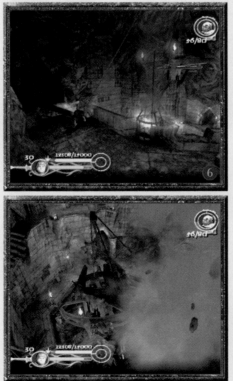

Cut the rope above and
cause havoc below.

A gang of Orcs rushes up the stairs to attack you. Spill the nearby brazier to even the odds and hack at the rest. Run down the stairs.

At the bottom circle, near where you dropped the chandelier and beyond the passage where you entered, is another archway. Go through, dispatching any Orcs you find there, and you'll be in the large open area. This is below the balcony where the hot oil cauldron was.

You're at ground level. Things have calmed down, thanks to your actions.

Farther along is more Orc squabble.

Press on until you come across another fierce battle scene. You can use your Elven Cloak to avoid most of it, but for the sake of experience points you may want to engage a few Orcs. Cull the mob by picking at the edges, engaging one foe at a time, and quickly dispatching them.

Eventually you come to another raised ramp and a winch that will send it down. Use the Action button to release it and crush the Orcs under the ramp. Clear away any stragglers, then head up.

You find another ramp and another group of Orcs underneath it. Bring the two together.

Do not stop. Pelt across the ruined bridge before it crumbles under your feet.

The other Orcs have run for the bridge, but the Champion stayed behind to watch over the ballista.

A quick shove and the barrels will topple into the crowd.

Follow the path and climb up the ladder at the end. You'll reach a platform holding a pair of Uruk-hai cheering a fight on a higher level. Sneak up and stab them, then look at the two barrels perched on the edge of the platform. Below is another large group of battling Orcs. Use your Action button to push the barrels onto them, clearing the area and gaining more experience points.

Go to the walkway where the pair of Uruk-hai was, and proceed up. The Orcs on the upper platform will flee to the tower and you'll be shown a ballista overlooking a stone bridge.

Move to the circular rampart holding the ballista. Climb up and use your Elven Cloak. An Orc Champion is up here, so sneak behind him and use your Finishing move for an Instant Kill.

DEVELOPER HINT

Don't delay once you've fired the Orc ballistae. Rush to Frodo!
—Michael Becker

When the Champion is out of the way, use your Action button to fire the ballista. It sends a huge chunk of wood crashing into the tower, which shatters and falls on the bridge. The Orcs are cleared away, but the bridge has been weakened.

Start moving when you fire the ballista. Get to the foot of the bridge and wait until the debris and Orcs have finished falling off. Run as fast as you can across the bridge and into the tower ahead. You'll be taken to the final segment of the level.

GORBAG'S ROOM

Climbing up a ladder, Sam finds a pair of Orcs fighting over Frodo's *mithril* shirt. Gorbag, the heartier creature, kills his opponent. To free Frodo, you must defeat this Orc.

Gorbag

Gorbag has an effective shield and a heavy sword. Your Fierce Attacks cannot shatter his defense. However, two sets of war pikes are available to help you fight the Orc.

You'll need to follow a process. Hit him with two war pikes, the second soon after the first. The initial pike will break Gorbag's shield. The second one will make him drop his sword.

At that point, his health bar comes up over his head. He's vulnerable when he's disarmed, so take advantage of the moment and use your attacks to whittle away at his health.

First take away his shield, then take away his sword. After that, strike hard and fast.

Most likely you'll only have time for one good combo. When Gorbag recovers, he'll rush to the weapon racks on the wall and re-arm himself for another attack. Hit him with two war pikes.

If you take too long between pikes, the Orc will regain a shield and you'll have to smash it again. However, throw the first pike, then Parry his rush before attempting to throw the second.

When his defenses are down, it's time to attack.

Before attempting to use the war pikes, take a little time to get used to Gorbag's attacks. You can Parry his strikes effectively, so let him make a few passes at you while you block. He swipes in twos and threes. Sometimes it will be three quick strikes or two quick and a third a second after. And once in a while, to keep you guessing, he'll swing two times. When you have a feel for his patterns, wait until he's done a three combo on you, then grab a war pike to start the battle.

When you defeat the Orc, a cutscene begins.

With Gorbag done for, Sam is able to rouse Frodo.

The other Orc wasn't killed, only stunned. He grabs Frodo's *mithril* shirt and flees.

Where he goes is a mystery. The hobbits now have to go to Mount Doom.

The Black Gates

Black Gates — Playing as Aragorn

Black Gates — Playing as Gandalf

Black Gates — Playing as Legolas

Black Gates — Playing as Gimli

The Path of the King

Characters: Aragorn, Legolas, Gimli, Gandalf
Enemies: Orcs, archer Orcs, Uruk-hai, Uruk-hai Champions, Orc Champions, Easterlings, Nazgûl

THE MOUTH OF SAURON

It comes to this.

The followers of Aragorn make their final stand at the Black Gates of Mordor. It is the last diversion to keep the Eye of Sauron from espying the Ring-bearer. It is a hopeless task, if Frodo should fail, but they must try.

The Mouth of Sauron comes forth to defend his gate. He says he has a token for the Armies of Men.

Frodo's *mithril* shirt is flung at their feet. Could the Ring-bearer have failed?

Whether or not the hobbit is dead, Aragorn must fight. And so he approaches the Mouth of Sauron.

Aragorn may step forward, but the actual character that battles the Mouth of Sauron depends on whom you choose to play. Whoever it is, the strategies remain the same.

The Mouth of Sauron

While he is an imposing opponent, the Mouth of Sauron has a simple (yet effective) range of attacks. He is first and foremost a swordsman and will use his skill to strike you with heavy blows.

Swordplay is the Mouth of Sauron's main strength.

The Mouth of Sauron will crouch and leap into the air, landing with a vicious overhand chop that is unblockable and knocks you to the ground. To avoid this, you must interrupt him. When he crouches, rush in for a Speed Attack. Otherwise, you'll end up on your back.

The crouch is the signal that the Mouth of Sauron is about to leap. When he comes down, his blow will tumble you to the ground.

Don't use your Ranged Attack; the shots are ineffective and bounce away from the Mouth of Sauron. Your Basic Attacks are useless, too. You can't trade Speed Attacks with this servant of Sauron. The upgrade moves and combos are an absolute necessity. You want to be able to hit him hard and fast enough so that his counterattacks are interrupted.

Unleash an unbroken string of Orc Hewers or Lightning Strikes against him, and you will get through the fight without much damage. The trick is to press the buttons accurately and fast. You may take a few hits, but pour out the combos and you'll hack chunks of health off of the Keeper's meter. Get in enough hits and the tall guardian will fall at your feet.

Combos are the way to win this battle.

Negotiations, as Gimli says, are over.

The real battle, however, is about to begin. The Black Gates swing wide to let out a stream of creatures bent on your destruction.

THE BATTLE

Now the real fight begins. The hordes of Mordor are rushing to dislodge the armies of men from a lone hill in the field. You have to defend it.

Depending on which character you are playing, your allies will be stationed at different points on the map. This will become important later on in the fight. Refer to the maps at the beginning of this section to see where everyone is placed.

Because the area you need to defend is small, you can quickly familiarize yourself with it. Ignore the enemies for a moment and look around. There are war pikes and fire braziers at three points on the map. The bulk of enemy forces will be entering the arena from the broken wall in the front.

Survey the area quickly, then brace yourself.

Kill the enemy Champions as fast as you can to progress quickly through the level stages.
—Michael Kirkbride

Notice the meter in the upper-right corner. You need to defeat six Orc Champions to move to the next stage of this level, and you'll have to defeat many more enemies in the meantime.

There really is no right way to progress in this battle. It is a free-for-all melee, so fight and Parry, destroying as many Orcs as you can.

You have one concern (beyond your own safety): the health of your companions. One after another, you'll see health meters for your friends appear at the top of the screen.

Playing as Aragorn, Gimli's is the first health meter to appear.

Monitor your friends' well-being. If they call for help or their vitality slips, find them. Fight off foes and stay close to your companion. He will glow and heal as you stick by. When he is healed, you can move about.

If any of your companions dies, you will lose the level. Keep a close watch on their meters and listen for cries for help.

During lulls in combat, always make sure to heal the other members of the Fellowship.
—Michael Kirkbride

Standing next to your wounded friends will heal them. Wait for the glow to surround them.

Archers can be a nuisance. Deal with them swiftly.

The first waves are numerous. Rove about and help in any crowded corner. Knock over braziers to delay and damage enemies. Do not let the Orc archers become too numerous. They usually stand by the front opening. Use your Ranged Attack against them, or charge and carve them away.

The first Orc Champion appears. His entrance is heralded by the appearance of a second health meter. Search around your three friends' positions; the Champions gravitate toward one of the principal characters.

A Champion is usually found fighting one of your companions.

The Champions drop health pick-ups when they are defeated.

During lulls in the action, mop up any remaining Orcs or tend to wounded friends. The calm won't last long; soon another wave will hit and you'll be back in the thick of it.

The second big wave includes Easterlings. They're tough, so don't go easy on them. Despite the chaos of the battle, you need to stay focused on specific enemies. While your allies will destroy a number of enemies without you, you can do it quickly. Go after one at a time, make sure you've dispatched him, then target the next one.

The Easterlings come in the second large assault on the hill.

The next Champion shows up, and the third health meter appears with him. Chase him down and use your Fierce Attacks or a war pike to strip him of his armor. If you smash away his defense, your friends will be able to damage him, too.

 Two war pikes will kill an Orc Champion: One breaks through his armor, and the second finishes the job.

The second Champion runs toward one of the Fellowship.

The third Champion follows closely after the second. Follow the same tactics you've been using. If the fighting is thick, knock away the Champion's armor, then clear the random Orcs clogging the area. When you

return to the Champion, your allies have damaged him. Soon after the third Champion falls, the fourth will come in for a similar welcome.

An Orc Champion without armor can be defeated without your help.

 Keep checking your friends' health. Make a circuit, visiting each for a short time as you battle back and forth across the arena.

After the fourth Champion is slain, the attackers will redouble their efforts and come at your position from three sides. This doesn't mean much. Just keep fighting them off, no matter where they come from.

The fifth Champion will hop over the wall to the east, so run over and deal with him. After you dispatch him, head to the front of the arena and deal with a line of Orc archers that will harm you unless they are cleared away.

Check out the opening to the west. Use your Ranged Attack to clear away any archers on the platform below. After they're gone, the fifth Orc Champion will come at you.

Stand by your companion on the raised ledge and fire at the Orcs below. Usually another Champion will join in.

The sixth Champion will follow quickly after the fifth. By now you should be expert at taking them down. Do so and you'll hit a **Checkpoint**, reaching the final stage of this level.

CHECKPOINT

THE NAZGÛL

The Ringwraiths fly in on Fell Beasts to deal with the upstarts on the hill.

Sauron's darkest minions stand to face the defenders.

The Ringwraiths are tough creatures, but you don't have to worry about hordes of Orcs getting in the way as you battle the Ringwraiths. The best start is to rush to the war pikes and hurl one into each of the Ringwraiths. They are vulnerable to fire, and a stab from one of the heated war pikes will make them susceptible to your Normal Attacks.

A war pike for each Nazgûl is essential at the start.

The Ringwraiths are going to wreak havoc on your companions, who pair up and leave you to your own devices. Do not wade in with your Melee Attacks. The best tactic is to use your Ranged Attack on these servants of Sauron. With all the upgrades you've purchased, your shots should be very powerful by now. And the Ringwraiths are vulnerable to your shots.

Stand back and fire at the nearest one. Concentrate on a single one until it goes down. The less enemies you have to deal with, the better off you'll be.

Your powerful Ranged Attacks will be effective against these opponents.

These foes will hit your friends hard. You may have to race to one's defense, standing nearby to heal him. Use your Ranged Attack while you heal your friend; be careful of the Nazgûl striking at you when you draw near.

Your first priority is to thin them out. Spear them with war pikes and then slay one with your Ranged Attack. If your companions are doing all right, go after a second one. If things are looking grim for your friends, move in to heal them. With luck you'll be able to stand so that two (or even all three) of them can be healed at the same time.

> **TIP**
> Slay a Nazgûl before your fellows scatter to different parts of the arena. It's difficult to reach them for healing if they're far away from you.

When you're down to one Nazgûl, it's possible to help all your companions at once.

Continue to fire your Ranged Attacks, paying attention to your health and that of your friends. When the final one falls, you will have completed the Black Gates level.

The fighting is almost over for the King and his companions. Now it all rests on Frodo and Sam.

Crack of Doom

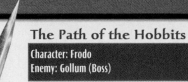

(Second)

(First)

start

Crack of Doom

The Path of the Hobbits

Character: Frodo
Enemy: Gollum (Boss)

THE LAST ACT

The final level is played with a new character, Frodo.

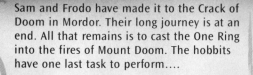

Sam and Frodo have made it to the Crack of Doom in Mordor. Their long journey is at an end. All that remains is to cast the One Ring into the fires of Mount Doom. The hobbits have one last task to perform....

Gollum

The fight against Gollum is tricky. However, after you get used to the creature's movements you will be able to succeed.

The goal is to get Gollum (and the One Ring) into the fires of Mount Doom. None of your Normal Attacks can harm Gollum. He will take no damage from your weapons. The best you can do is herd the poor creature toward the edge with your strikes but even that is limited. When Gollum is attacking or shrieking, you can't budge him. The only times you can effect his movements with your attacks is when he's cowering (bent almost double with one arm over his head) or when he's down on all fours.

When Gollum cowers, you can swipe at him to make him move.

DEVELOPER HINT

When you see Gollum do a backflip, you've got him on the run: Speed Attacks will cause him to jump backward and to the right. Using Fierce Attacks will cause him to jump backward and to the left. This can help you guide him toward the edge. —Bret Robbins

A more efficient way to get Gollum to the edge is to let him get there himself. You can't fall off, so hug the rim of the platform and wait for Gollum to jump at you. The timing needs to be right: You don't want him to collide with you. As soon as you see him jump or charge toward you, move out of the way.

This is all in an effort to get Gollum to the edge of the rock platform you're on. When he's close, dodge around so he's between you and the edge and use an attack to get him teetering. You'll see his arms pinwheel as he tries to keep his balance.

Maneuver Gollum so he's poised, unbalanced, on the lip of the platform. Shove him over, then use your Killing move to knock him off.

Use your Kick button to shove him off. The creature hangs onto the edge, wailing. Stand over him and use your Killing move. This sends Gollum into the pit, damaging his health bar. But he's not finished, so be wary.

DEVELOPER HINT

The bridge is a safety zone from Gollum and the falling hazards. However, Gollum won't go on the bridge himself, so you won't beat the level by hanging out there. —Bret Robbins

The crafty Gollum clings to the rock face and climbs up. Mount Doom, meanwhile, is getting unstable. Rocks start smashing down on the platform.

The platform is a dangerous place to stand.

You won't get caught in the rock slide, but it makes the platform more cramped.

Lure Gollum to the edge and perform the same sequence. Strike at him to get him off-balance, use your Kick to push him over the edge, then use the Killing move to knock him off. As Gollum makes his way to the platform, more rocks crash down. Soon, Gollum will have reached you, so be prepared for another encounter. A red health vial appears opposite the bridge: Grab it if you need it.

After the third time you knock Gollum off, the mountain responds by sending lava onto the platform. Stick to the edges to avoid the hot magma and wait for your opponent to reappear. When he's back, repeat your pattern. Lure him to the edge and get him off it.

After you do this, a portion of the platform shears away into the lava below. You now have a smaller area in which to avoid Gollum. It makes you more vulnerable to his attacks because he can reach you quicker. However, stick to the lip of the platform and continue luring and dodging to get him off the edge.

After Gollum goes down another time, the platform becomes a maelstrom of falling rocks and lava. Move along the edge to avoid the worst of it. If you take damage, a red health vial appears near the bridge. Only one more knockdown to go.

The mountain seems to know the end is near.

For the final round, the pattern is the same: Bring Gollum to the edge, dodge out of the way, and attack to get him teetering. Use your Kick button to push him over, then use your Killing move. You'll start a cutscene as Gollum goes down for the final time.

After withstanding Gollum's Fierce Attacks, a health bonus is a welcome sight.

NOTE

That is not, however, the end of your game. There are secrets to explore and new characters to play. Read the sealed section to find out what you've unlocked.

THE LORD OF THE RINGS

THE RETURN OF THE KING

EA GAMES

PRIMA
GAMES

THE LORD OF THE RINGS

THE RETURN OF THE KING

SEALED SECTION

Secrets

There are several unlockable features in *The Lord of the Rings: The Return of the King* game. Some will be found as you progress through the levels, but the big payoff comes when you finish the game. You'll find several new features at the top of the level map, above the tree.

The top of the level map, home of your prizes.

VIDEO FEATURES

As you play the game, you'll be rewarded with numerous video features. Actors from the films (who also provide voices for the game) appear in several exclusive interviews. Plus, you'll find video slide shows of art for the film and the game itself. Highly enjoyable and found nowhere else, these secrets are unveiled on the level tree. They appear as small glowing dots in between the icons for the levels.

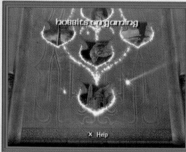

There's a video selection dot to the right of the Helm's Deep level icon. Use your movement control to highlight them.

Accessing the video clips depends on how far you've gone in the game. Here's a table showing what you can find and what level you must complete to find it. For example, you can't see the game concept art slide show until you've successfully completed Paths of the Dead.

Unlockable Video Features

VIDEO TITLE	MUST COMPLETE
Film Concept Art	Helm's Deep
Hobbits on Gaming	Helm's Deep
Game Concept Art	Paths of the Dead
Christopher Lee Interview	The Road to Isengard
Sean Astin Interview	Escape from Osgiliath
Film Production Stills	The Southern Gate
Ian McKellen Interview	Minas Tirith—Top of the Wall
Elijah Wood Interview	Shelob's Lair
Billy Boyd Interview	The Crack of Doom
Dom Monaghan Interview	The Crack of Doom
Andy Serkis Interview	The Crack of Doom
David Wenham Interview	The Crack of Doom

NEW CHARACTERS

When you reach the Crack of Doom level, you'll have unlocked Frodo as a playable character. After finishing the game, you can replay the game with any character on any level (except for Helm's Deep).

So, if you want to see how Legolas fares in Osgiliath, or how Faramir might hold up on the Road to Isengard, you can find out. Here is a quick rundown of the four new characters so you know what to expect from them as you play.

Frodo

In the final days of the War of the Ring, the fate of all Middle-earth rests in the hands of Frodo Baggins. Now upon the most difficult part of his long journey, Frodo and his trusted companion Sam at last approach the devastated land of Mordor, home of the Dark Lord Sauron. With every step taken toward that fell place, the burden upon Frodo grows heavier.

Relentlessly pursued by Ringwraiths mounted upon huge flying beasts, Frodo and Sam must trust Gollum, if they hope to find safe passage through the encircling orc forces. While huge armies rage around them, these two small hobbits must never falter, for failure will bring about the ruin of the world.

Although Frodo is an unlockable character, playing as Frodo is vital to the completion of the game. He is the character you use in the Crack of Doom level the first time around.

Frodo, like all the hobbits, is almost identical to Sam in his playing style. He is quicker, but Frodo nonetheless needs to be handled in the same way as Sam. When you get to control him in the initial play-through at the Crack of Doom level, Frodo is only at Level 1. This is sufficient to defeat Gollum (as outlined in the walkthrough), but you don't have access to any of the upgrades until the hobbit reaches Level 2.

When you play again with Frodo, refer to the analysis of Sam in the Characters section of this guide. Frodo's moves and style are the same.

Pippin

In the uniform of a soldier of Gondor, Pippin is a hobbit who has learned to take care of himself. As with his fellows, his talents lie not in great strength, but in speed and guile. However, he is quite able to take care of himself in a battlefield situation.

The analysis for Sam can be applied to Pippin (it works for all the hobbits), so read that piece in the Characters section of this guide.

Merry

Clad in the garb of the Rohirrim, Merry is stout on the battlefield and true to his friends. Like the other hobbits from the Shire, Merry isn't a bruiser of a character, but he manages to get by.

Use Sam's information in the Characters section of this guide to inform you on how to approach play with Merry.

Upgrade Chart

Character	Link 1	Link 2	Link 3	Devastating 2	Devastating 3	Devastating 4	Ranged 2	Ranged 3	Ranged 4	Ranged 5	Combo 1	Combo 2	Combo 3	Combo 4	Combo 5
Faramir	Orc Bane	Warrior Bane	Bane of Sauron	Ranger Fury	Wilderness Rage	Wrath of Númenor	Dúnedain Arrows	Rivendell Arrows	Mithril Arrows	N/A	Orc Hewer	Final Judgment	Balrog's Gambit	Dark Deliverance	Shield Cleaver
Merry/Pippin	Orc Bane	Warrior Bane	Bane of Sauron	Poison Blade	Cloud of Shadow	Cloud of Rage	Poison Daggers	Morgul Daggers	N/A	N/A	Orc Hewer	Final Judgment	Balrog's Gambit	Dark Deliverance	Shield Cleaver
Faramir Cost	5,000	7,000	9,000	4,000	5,000	7,000	5,000	5,500	7,000	N/A	1,000	5,000	5,000	7,000	7,000
Faramir Level	2	5	7	2	4	6	3	6	8	N/A	2	2	4	5	6
Merry Cost	5,000	7,000	9,000	4,000	5,000	7,000	5,500	7,000	N/A	N/A	1,000	5,000	5,000	7,000	7,000
Merry Level	2	4	6	3	5	9	5	7	N/A	N/A	2	2	4	5	6
Pippin Cost	5,000	7,000	9,000	4,000	5,000	7,000	5,500	7,000	N/A	N/A	1,000	5,000	5,000	7,000	7,000
Pippin Level	2	4	6	3	5	9	5	7	N/A	N/A	2	2	4	5	6
Fellowship Cost	8,000	10,000	12,000	N/A	N/A	N/A	N/A	N/A	N/A	N/A	3,000	8,000	8,000	11,000	11,000

Faramir

Prince of Gondor and one of the few men who successfully resisted the lure of The One Ring, Faramir is the last of the unlockable characters. His moves and upgrades are nearly identical to those of Aragorn, and you can play Faramir in much the same way as the son of Arathorn. Read the section on Aragorn in the Characters section of this guide to get a feel for how to approach playing as Faramir.

The notable exception is that Faramir is a stronger bowman than Aragorn. His Ranged Attacks are very powerful. Charge them up and let fly to wreak havoc among your enemies.

Combo 6	Combo 7	Combo 8	Ability 1	Ability 2	Ability 3	Health 1	Health 2	Health 3	Health 4	Health 5	Damage 1	Perfect	Rising
Lightning Strike	Helm's Hammer	Swift Justice	Gondorian Sword Master	Kingmaker	N/A	Strength of Stone	Strength of Iron	Strength of the Fellowship	Strength of the Evenstar	N/A	Sword Mastery of Kings	Killing Zone	Rising Revenge
Lightning Strike	Helm's Hammer	Swift Justice	Cloak of Haldir	Cloak of Celeborn	Cloak of Galadriel	Strength of Stone	Strength of Iron	Strength of the Fellowship	Halfling Strength	Baggins Strength	Strength of the Gaffer	Killing Zone	Rising Revenge
7,000	12,000	12,000	3,500	7,000	N/A	5,000	5,000	5,000	5,000	N/A	25,000	10,000	10,000
8	9	10	3	7	N/A	3	5	6	10	N/A	10	8	3
7,000	12,000	12,000	3,500	7,000	10,500	5,000	5,000	5,000	5,000	5,000	25,000	10,000	10,000
8	9	10	3	6	10	3	5	7	8	10	10	8	3
7,000	12,000	12,000	3,500	7,000	10,500	5,000	5,000	5,000	5,000	5,000	25,000	10,000	10,000
8	9	10	3	6	10	3	5	7	8	10	10	8	3
11,000	20,000	20,000	N/A	N/A	N/A	15,000	15,000	15,000	N/A	N/A	N/A	20,000	20,000

SECRET CODES

Here is a list of secret codes that you'll be able to use in *The Lord of the Rings: The Return of the King*. This chart covers multiple platforms.

You must finish the game to be able to use these codes.

For the console games, follow the instructions below before entering the code string:

> 1. **PAUSE THE GAME SO THE OPTIONS MENU APPEARS.**
> 2. **HOLD DOWN ALL SHOULDER BUTTONS AT ONCE.**
> 3. **ENTER THE CODE WITH SHOULDER BUTTONS STILL DEPRESSED.**

When you've entered the code correctly you'll hear a sound that indicates success.

 If you want to enter more than one code, release the shoulder buttons, then hold them down again before entering each code.

In the secret codes chart, you'll see several codes listed as "one-time use." This doesn't necessarily mean you can only use them once. Codes such as "Restore Missiles" can be entered each time you need to fill up your Ranged-Attack Ammunition.

The codes marked "on/off" indicate codes whose effects are continuous and can be turned on or off. Codes such as "Invulnerability" are on and off. You can reverse them after you've turned them on by entering the code again.

Secret Codes

Code	Usage	Character	PS2 Combo	Xbox Combo	GameCube Combo	PC Combo
+1,000 Experience Points	one-time use	Gimli	●,●,▲,×	B,B,Y,A	X,X,Y,A	5,5,6,4
+1,000 Experience Points	one-time use	Gandalf	●,▲,↑,↓	B,Y,Y,A	X,Y,↑,X	5,6,8,9
+1,000 Experience Points	one-time use	Merry	↓,↓,■,×	Y,Y,X,A	X,X,B,A	9,9,7,4
+1,000 Experience Points	one-time use	Frodo	↓,▲,↑,↓	Y,Y,Y,A	X,Y,↑,X	9,6,8,9
+1,000 Experience Points	one-time use	Faramir	■,▲,↑,■	X,Y,Y,X	B,Y,↑,B	7,6,8,7
+1,000 Experience Points	one-time use	Aragorn	↑,■,▲,×	Y,X,Y,A	↑,B,Y,A	8,7,6,4
+1,000 Experience Points	one-time use	Sam	▲,×,↓,×	Y,A,Y,A	Y,A,X,A	6,4,9,4
+1,000 Experience Points	one-time use	Pippin	▲,×,■,×	Y,A,X,A	Y,A,B,A	6,4,7,4
+1,000 Experience Points	one-time use	Legolas	×,▲,↑,×	A,Y,Y,A	A,Y,↑,A	4,6,8,4
Level 2 Skills	on/off	Merry	●,↓,■,■	B,Y,X,X	X,X,B,B	5,9,7,7
Level 2 Skills	on/off	Aragorn	●,▲,×,▲	B,Y,A,Y	X,Y,A,Y	5,6,4,6
Level 2 Skills	on/off	Sam	●,×,●,▲	B,A,B,Y	X,A,X,Y	5,4,5,6
Level 2 Skills	on/off	Gandalf	↓,▲,×,▲	Y,Y,A,Y	X,Y,A,Y	9,6,4,6
Level 2 Skills	on/off	Pippin	↓,×,↓,↑	Y,A,Y,↑	X,A,X,↑	9,4,9,8
Level 2 Skills	on/off	Legolas	■,■,●,■	X,X,B,X	B,B,X,B	7,7,5,7
Level 2 Skills	on/off	Gimli	↑,●,■,■	Y,B,X,X	↑,X,B,B	8,5,7,7
Level 2 Skills	on/off	Frodo	▲,↑,↓,●	Y,Y,Y,B	Y,↑,X,X	6,8,9,5
Level 2 Skills	on/off	Faramir	×,■,×,↓	A,X,A,Y	A,B,A,X	4,7,4,9
Level 4 Skills	on/off	Legolas	↓,↓,×,×	Y,Y,A,A	X,X,A,A	9,9,4,4
Level 4 Skills	on/off	Aragorn	↓,■,●,■	Y,X,B,X	X,B,X,B	9,7,5,7
Level 4 Skills	on/off	Merry	■,×,●,↓	X,A,B,Y	B,A,X,X	7,4,5,9
Level 4 Skills	on/off	Sam	↑,↓,■,×	Y,Y,X,A	↑,X,B,A	8,9,7,4

Code	Usage	Character	PS2 Combo	Xbox Combo	GameCube Combo	PC Combo
Level 4 Skills	on/off	Gimli	▲,■,↓,↑	Y,X,A,B	Y,B,X,↑	6,7,9,8
Level 4 Skills	on/off	Frodo	▲,↑,●,↓	Y,A,B,A	Y,↑,B,X	6,8,5,9
Level 4 Skills	on/off	Gandalf	▲,↑,■,✕	Y,A,X,A	Y,↑,B,A	6,8,7,4
Level 4 Skills	on/off	Pippin	✕,↓,↓,↓	A,B,B,B	A,X,X,X	4,9,9,9
Level 4 Skills	on/off	Faramir	✕,✕,■,■	A,A,X,X	A,A,B,B	4,4,7,7
Restore Missiles	one-time use	Gimli	●,●,●,✕	B,B,B,A	X,X,X,A	5,5,5,4
Restore Missiles	one-time use	Merry	■,●,●,▲	X,B,B,Y	B,X,X,Y	7,5,5,6
Restore Missiles	one-time use	Pippin	↑,●,↓,■	A,B,B,X	↑,X,X,B	8,5,9,7
Restore Missiles	one-time use	Gandalf	▲,↓,✕,■	Y,B,A,X	Y,X,A,B	6,9,4,7
Restore Missiles	one-time use	Aragorn	▲,■,■,▲	Y,X,X,Y	Y,B,B,Y	6,7,7,6
Restore Missiles	one-time use	Faramir	▲,↑,✕,✕	Y,A,A,A	Y,↑,A,A	6,8,4,4
Restore Missiles	one-time use	Legolas	▲,▲,▲,↓	Y,Y,Y,B	Y,Y,Y,X	6,6,6,9
Restore Missiles	one-time use	Frodo	▲,▲,▲,●	Y,Y,Y,B	Y,Y,Y,X	6,6,6,5
Restore Missiles	one-time use	Sam	✕,✕,●,✕	A,A,B,A	A,A,X,A	4,4,5,4
Unlock 3 Hit Combo for	on/off	Gandalf	↓,✕,▲,↓	B,A,Y,B	X,A,Y,X	9,4,6,9
Unlock 3 Hit Combo for	on/off	Aragorn	■,↓,●,↑	X,B,B,A	B,X,X,↑	7,9,5,8
Unlock 3 Hit Combo for	on/off	Frodo	■,↓,▲,■	X,B,Y,X	B,X,Y,B	7,9,6,7
Unlock 3 Hit Combo for	on/off	Faramir	■,▲,↑,▲	X,Y,A,Y	B,Y,↑,Y	7,6,8,6
Unlock 3 Hit Combo for	on/off	Legolas	■,▲,▲,●	X,Y,Y,B	B,Y,Y,X	7,6,6,5
Unlock 3 Hit Combo for	on/off	Sam	■,✕,●,■	X,A,B,X	B,A,X,B	7,4,5,7
Unlock 3 Hit Combo for	on/off	Gimli	↑,■,●,■	A,X,B,X	↑,B,X,B	8,7,5,7
Unlock 3 Hit Combo for	on/off	Pippin	↑,↑,■,●	A,A,X,B	↑,↑,B,X	8,8,7,5
Unlock 3 Hit Combo for	on/off	Merry	▲,✕,↑,▲	Y,A,A,Y	Y,A,↑,Y	6,4,8,6
Unlock Secret Character	one-time use	Frodo	▲,●,●,●	Y,B,B,B	Y,X,X,X	6,5,5,5
All Experience you get, your buddy gets	on/off	Co-op	↓,✕,✕,✕	B,A,A,A	X,A,A,A	9,4,4,4
All Health you get, your buddy gets	on/off	Co-op	▲,↑,■,■	Y,A,X,X	Y,↑,B,B	6,8,7,7
Level 6 Skills	on/off	Pippin	●,▲,●,▲	B,Y,B,Y	X,Y,X,Y	5,6,5,6
Level 6 Skills	on/off	Aragorn	●,▲,■,■	B,Y,X,X	X,Y,B,B	5,6,7,7
Level 6 Skills	on/off	Legolas	↓,●,↑,↓	B,B,A,B	X,X,↑,X	9,5,8,9
Level 6 Skills	on/off	Merry	↓,↓,■,▲	B,B,X,Y	X,X,B,Y	9,9,7,6
Level 6 Skills	on/off	Sam	↓,↓,↑,↑	B,B,A,A	X,X,↑,↑	9,9,8,8
Level 6 Skills	on/off	Frodo	↓,↓,✕,▲	B,B,A,Y	X,X,A,Y	9,9,4,6
Level 6 Skills	on/off	Gimli	↓,▲,↓,■	B,Y,B,X	X,Y,X,B	9,6,9,7
Level 6 Skills	on/off	Gandalf	▲,▲,✕,↑	Y,Y,A,A	Y,Y,A,↑	6,6,4,8

THE LORD OF THE RINGS
THE RETURN OF THE KING
PRIMA'S OFFICIAL STRATEGY GUIDE

Code	Usage	Character	PS2 Combo	Xbox Combo	GameCube Combo	PC Combo
Level 6 Skills	on/off	Faramir	▲,✕,↓,●	Y,A,X,B	Y,A,Y,X	6,4,9,5
Level 8 Skills	on/off	Frodo	●,●,↓,↓	B,B,X,X	X,X,X,X	5,5,9,9
Level 8 Skills	on/off	Sam	●,●,▲,▲	B,B,Y,Y	X,X,Y,Y	5,5,6,6
Level 8 Skills	on/off	Faramir	●,↓,↓,↓	B,X,X,X	X,X,X,X	5,9,9,9
Level 8 Skills	on/off	Gandalf	●,■,↓,↓	B,X,X,X	X,B,X,X	5,7,9,9
Level 8 Skills	on/off	Merry	↓,▲,✕,■	X,Y,A,X	X,Y,A,B	9,6,4,7
Level 8 Skills	on/off	Legolas	■,↑,↑,↓	X,↑,↑,X	B,↑,↑,X	7,8,8,9
Level 8 Skills	on/off	Pippin	■,↑,↑,●	X,↑,↑,B	B,↑,↑,B	7,8,8,5
Level 8 Skills	on/off	Aragorn	↑,■,▲,↑	↑,X,Y,↑	↑,B,Y,↑	8,7,6,8
Level 8 Skills	on/off	Gimli	✕,●,↓,■	A,B,X,X	A,X,X,B	4,5,9,7
Unlock 4 Hit Combo for	on/off	Frodo	↓,■,↓,●	X,X,X,B	X,B,X,X	9,7,9,5
Unlock 4 Hit Combo for	on/off	Gandalf	↓,▲,↑,●	X,Y,X,B	X,Y,↑,X	9,6,8,5
Unlock 4 Hit Combo for	on/off	Merry	■,✕,■,■	X,A,X,X	B,A,B,B	7,4,7,7
Unlock 4 Hit Combo for	on/off	Sam	↑,↓,▲,▲	X,X,Y,Y	↑,X,Y,Y	8,9,6,6
Unlock 4 Hit Combo for	on/off	Aragorn	↑,■,▲,↓	X,X,Y,X	↑,B,Y,X	8,7,6,9
Unlock 4 Hit Combo for	on/off	Gimli	▲,■,↑,✕	Y,X,X,A	Y,B,↑,A	6,7,8,4
Unlock 4 Hit Combo for	on/off	Legolas	✕,●,▲,■	A,B,Y,X	A,X,Y,B	4,5,6,7
Unlock 4 Hit Combo for	on/off	Faramir	✕,■,↑,✕	A,X,X,A	A,B,↑,A	4,7,8,4
Unlock 4 Hit Combo for	on/off	Pippin	✕,✕,↓,●	A,A,X,B	A,A,X,X	4,4,9,5
Unlock All Actor Interviews	one-time use	Special Features	✕,■,✕,↑	A,X,A,X	A,B,A,↑	4,7,4,8
Unlock Secret Character	one-time use	Frodo	●,■,■,✕	B,X,X,A	X,B,B,A	5,7,7,4
Unlock Secret Character	one-time use	Pippin	▲,●,■,↓	Y,B,X,X	Y,X,B,X	6,5,7,9
Unlock Secret Character	one-time use	Merry	✕,↓,↓,✕	A,X,X,A	A,X,X,A	4,9,9,4
Unlock Secret Character	one-time use	Faramir	✕,✕,▲,▲	A,A,Y,Y	A,A,Y,Y	4,4,6,6
Unlock Special Abilities for	on/off	Gimli	●,■,✕,●	B,X,A,B	X,B,A,X	5,7,4,5
Unlock Special Abilities for	on/off	Aragorn	↓,●,▲,▲	X,B,Y,Y	X,X,Y,Y	9,5,6,6
Unlock Special Abilities for	on/off	Pippin	■,✕,●,▲	X,A,B,Y	B,A,X,Y	7,4,5,6
Unlock Special Abilities for	on/off	Sam	↑,●,✕,●	X,B,A,B	↑,X,A,X	8,5,4,5
Unlock Special Abilities for	on/off	Gandalf	↑,↓,▲,●	X,X,Y,B	↑,X,Y,X	8,9,6,5
Unlock Special Abilities for	on/off	Faramir	↑,■,●,↑	X,X,B,X	↑,B,X,↑	8,7,5,8
Unlock Special Abilities for	on/off	Merry	↑,▲,●,●	X,Y,B,B	↑,Y,X,X	8,6,5,5
Unlock Special Abilities for	on/off	Legolas	▲,●,✕,●	Y,B,A,B	Y,X,A,X	6,5,4,5
Unlock Special Abilities for	on/off	Frodo	▲,✕,↓,✕	Y,A,X,A	Y,A,X,A	6,4,9,4
Infinite Re-spawns for Co-op	on/off	All	●,■,↑,●	B,X,X,B	X,B,↑,X	5,7,8,5
All Upgrades	one-time use	Any Character	↑,↓,▲,■	X,X,Y,X	↑,X,Y,B	8,9,6,7
Always Devastating	on/off	Any Character	▲,↑,▲,↓	Y,X,Y,X	Y,↑,Y,X	6,8,6,9
Infinite Missiles	on/off	Any Character	■,■,↓,●	X,X,X,B	B,B,X,X	7,7,9,5
Invulnerable	on/off	Any Character	■,●,■,↑	X,B,X,X	B,X,B,↑	7,5,7,8
Perfect Mode	on/off	Any Character	●,↓,▲,✕	B,X,Y,A	X,X,Y,A	5,9,6,4
Targeting Indicator Mode	on/off	Any Character	↓,●,↑,■	X,B,X,X	X,X,↑,B	9,5,8,7
Restore Health	one-time use	Any Character	■,■,●,●	X,X,B,B	B,B,X,X	7,7,5,5

THE PALANTÍR ARENAS

The *palantír* arenas are 20-level battle arenas that pit your character against waves of enemies. The sheer weight of numbers gives your foes the advantage, but you have experience on your side.

Don't take characters through the *palantír* arenas until they reach Level 10. That will ensure that you've maxed out their upgrades before throwing them into the pit.

 You'll need to defeat both *palantír* arenas to achieve 100 percent completion of the game.

At the beginning of each level (except the first), you'll be given a red health vial. If you don't use it on that level, it will carry over to the next one. After every five levels, you'll be given a Ranged-Attack Ammunition pick-up.

The key word for dealing with a *palantír* is patience. As things get crazier, you can find yourself trying to bash your way through without pausing for thought or Parries. Here are some hints.

- TAKE THE TIME TO LOOK AT THE TABLES PROVIDED HERE TO FIND OUT WHAT YOU'RE GOING TO BE FACING.

- PARRY LIKE YOU'VE NEVER PARRIED BEFORE. IF IT TAKES SIX PARRIES FOR ONE ATTACK TO STAY SAFE, DO IT. YOU'VE GOT A LONG WAY TO GO.

- HARBOR YOUR RANGED ATTACKS. USE THEM SPARINGLY AS YOU GO AND MAKE SURE YOU HIT THE LAST FEW LEVELS WITH A FULL QUIVER.

- KEEP FOOT SOLDIERS BETWEEN YOU AND ARCHERS (IF POSSIBLE). THE MELEE FOES WILL SOAK UP SOME OF THE ARROWS SHOT AT YOU.

- WHEN FACED WITH MOBS OF SHIELDED ENEMIES, USE YOUR FIERCE ATTACK TO SMASH AS MANY SHIELDS AS POSSIBLE BEFORE FOCUSING ON INDIVIDUAL ENEMIES. SHIELDS WILL STOP YOUR COMBOS.

- IF YOU SEE A TROLL, TAKE IT DOWN QUICKLY. USE YOUR RANGED ATTACKS TO DROP IT.

- GANDALF'S SPECIAL ABILITY IS A GREAT BOON IN THE LATER LEVELS, BUT YOU HAVE TO ACTIVATE IT RIGHT AT THE BEGINNING. SINCE IT TAKES SO LONG TO DEVELOP, YOU CAN BE INTERRUPTED BY ATTACKING MONSTERS LATER ON IN THE LEVEL.

- BECOME EXPERT AT USING YOUR LINK MOVE. IT WORKS OFF OF A PARRY, SO YOU CAN KEEP YOURSELF SAFE AND DESTROY AN ENEMY WITH ONE MOVE. PLUS, IT PUTS YOU IMMEDIATELY INTO PERFECT MODE. THAT'S A GOOD MOVE ALL AROUND.

- ALL THE ARENAS HAVE STRUCTURES IN THE MIDDLE OF THEIR CIRCULAR AREA. SOME OF THESE OBJECTS BLOCK ARROWS, OTHERS DON'T. USE THE CENTRAL OBJECTS FOR COVER WHEN YOU CAN.

- IF YOU'RE IN A CROWD AND CAN'T ATTACK BECAUSE OF ALL THE BLOWS RAINING DOWN ON YOU, USE YOUR KICK MOVE TO BURST THROUGH. THEN RUN TO SPREAD OUT YOUR OPPONENTS SO YOU CAN DEAL WITH THEM IN SMALLER CLUSTERS.

The *palantír* of Sauron is the more difficult of the two. The number of enemies is greater per level and the monsters are stronger. In order to open it, you must have at least one character from each of the three paths at Level 10 or higher. In other words, Gandalf, Sam, and either Aragorn, Legolas, or Gimli must be at the tenth level.

Here is a pair of lists showing what opponents you'll face on each level of the *palantír* arenas. Check them out so it won't be a surprise when 30 spiders charge you. Knowing what's ahead can help you formulate a plan of attack. Being forewarned will save you those few seconds of confusion as you try to figure out what you're up against.

The *Palantír* of Saruman

Level 1
14 dead soldiers

Level 2
14 Uruk-hai, red health vial

Level 3
7 dead soldiers, 7 Uruk-hai, red health vial

Level 4
8 dead soldier archers, red health vial

Level 5

7 Uruk-hai archers,
red health vial

Level 6

5 Uruk-hai archers,
5 dead soldier
archers, red health
vial, ranged ammo

Level 7

6 shielded dead
soldiers,
red health vial

Level 8

6 shielded
Uruk-hai,
red health vial

Level 9

4 shielded Uruk-
hai, 4 shielded
dead soldiers,
red health vial

Level 10

6 dead soldiers,
6 Uruk-hai archers,
red health vial

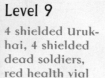

Level 11

3 huge spiders,
30 large spiders,
red health vial,
ranged ammo

Secrets

Level 12

6 shielded
dead soldiers,
5 Uruk-hai archers,
red health vial

Level 13

6 shielded
Uruk-hai,
5 dead soldier
archers,
red health vial

Level 14

4 Uruk-hai,
4 shielded dead
soldiers,
4 dead soldier
archers,
red health vial

Level 15

6 shielded Uruk-
hai, 4 dead
soldiers, 3 dead
soldier archers,
red health vial

Level 16

5 dead soldier
Champions,
red health vial,
ranged ammo

Level 17

4 Uruk-hai
Champions,
red health vial

Level 18

4 trolls, 20 spiders,
red health vial

Level 19

3 shielded Uruk-hai, 1 troll, 2 dead soldier Champions, 3 spiders, red health vial

Level 20

2 trolls, 3 dead soldier Champions, 4 dead soldier archers, 3 spiders, 3 shielded Uruk-hai, red health vial, ranged ammo

The *Palantír* of Sauron

Level 1

24 Orcs

Level 2

28 Easterlings, red health vial

Level 3

14 Orcs, 14 Easterlings

Secrets

Level 4

16 Orc archers, red health vial

Level 5

14 Uruk-hai crossbows, red health vial

Level 6

10 Uruk-hai crossbows, 10 Orc archers, red health vial, ranged ammo

Level 7

12 shielded Uruk-hai, red health vial

Level 8

12 shielded Easterlings, red health vial

Level 9

8 shielded Uruk-hai, 8 shielded Easterlings, red health vial

Level 10

12 Orcs, 12 Uruk-hai crossbows, red health vial

Level 11

5 Orc archers, 16 Easterlings, red health vial, ranged ammo

Level 14

8 Orc archers, 8 Easterlings, 8 shielded Uruk-hai, red health vial

Level 12

10 Uruk-hai crossbows, 10 shielded Uruk-hai, red health vial

Level 15

6 Orc archers, 8 Orcs, 12 shielded Easterlings, red health vial

Level 13

10 Orc archers, 12 shielded Easterlings, red health vial

Level 16

6 Uruk-hai Berserkers, red health vial, ranged ammo

Secrets

Level 17

6 Easterling Champions, red health vial

Level 18

4 Uruk-hai Berserkers, 3 Easterling Champions, troll, red health vial

Level 19

6 Uruk-hai Berserkers, 4 Easterling Champions, troll, red health vial

Level 20

6 Orc archers, 8 Uruk-hai Berserkers, 6 Easterling Champions, 2 trolls, red health vial, ranged ammo

THE LORD OF THE RINGS
THE RETURN OF THE KING

SEALED SECTION